KT-1-144-194

The **NO-NONSENSE GUIDE** to

FAIR TRADE

London

About the author
Sally Blundell is a freelance journalist and editor living in Christchurch, New Zealand/Aotearoa. She writes for a number of magazines in New Zealand and, in 2007, edited *Look This Way: New Zealand writers on New Zealand artists* (AUP), which was shortlisted for the Montana New Zealand Book Awards. She has also undertaken research and publication work for the NZ fair trade organization Trade Aid. In 2011, she was one of a group hosted by Tara Projects in Delhi, India. In 2013, she wrote a history of Trade Aid to coincide with the organization's 40th anniversary.

Acknowledgements
Many thanks to Chris Brazier and the staff of New Internationalist for their patient and informed editing and commissioning. Thanks too to the staff of Trade Aid, New Zealand/Aotearoa, for their unceasing support and feedback, and to those managers and co-ordinators of fair trade organizations across the globe who never fail to translate the experiences of their diverse memberships for a remote readership.

About the New Internationalist
New Internationalist is an independent, not-for-profit publishing co-operative that reports on issues of global justice. We publish informative current affairs and popular reference titles, complemented by multicultural recipe books, photography and fiction from the Global South, as well as calendars, diaries and cards – all with a global justice world view.

If you like this *No-Nonsense Guide* you will also enjoy the *New Internationalist* magazine. The magazine is packed full of high-quality writing and in-depth analysis, including:
- The Big Story: understanding the key global issues
- The Facts: accessible infographics
- Agenda: cutting-edge reports
- Country profile: essential insights and star ratings
- Argument: heated debate between experts
- Mixed Media: the best of global culture.

To find out more about the **New Internationalist,** visit our website at
newint.org

The NO-NONSENSE GUIDE to
FAIR TRADE

Sally Blundell

NewInternationalist

The No-Nonsense Guide to Fair Trade
Published in the UK in 2013 by New Internationalist™ Publications Ltd
55 Rectory Road
Oxford OX4 1BW, UK
newint.org

Cover image: Ton Koene

Series editor: Chris Brazier
Design by New Internationalist Publications Ltd.

Printed in UK by TJ International Limited, Cornwall UK
who hold environmental accreditation ISO 14001.

British Library Cataloguing-in-Publication Data.
A catalogue record for this book is available from the British Library.

Library of Congress Cataloguing-in-Publication Data.
A catalogue for this book is available from the Library of Congress.

ISBN 978-1-78026-133-1

Foreword

I WRITE this foreword from the spice gardens of northern Karnataka, India, a region renowned as the Pepper Queen. It is in the region of the Western Ghats, from Karnataka to Kerala, where the spices – pepper, cardamom, clove, nutmeg and mace – grow alongside areca nut, coconut, banana, fruits and vegetables.

As Sally Blundell reminds us, it was the spices of India that Columbus was looking for when he landed in the Americas. We now have the narrative that Columbus 'discovered' America, instead of the more accurate narrative that he landed in the wrong place.

We also have the associated narrative that trade based on colonization, exploitation and slavery is 'free trade'. The British East India Company signed a free trade agreement in 1711 with the Mughal emperor, Faruksheer, which created unfair terms of trade and allowed the East India Company not just to take over our trade in silks and spices but also to become rulers of India.

The first freedom movement of 1857 got rid of the East India Company and the British Crown took over. Our second freedom movement told the British to quit India in 1942, and by 1947 we were politically independent. As former colonies became independent, they tried to correct the distortions in trade that colonization had introduced. Hence we see in Sally's guide that the share of farmers and producers kept increasing up to the 1970s when the new 'East India companies' started to undermine the gains producers had made. They organized to push new 'free trade' rules for themselves, and achieved it through the General Agreement in Trade and Tariffs (GATT) which led to the formation of the World Trade Organization.

For the last three decades I have been engaged with

movements resisting the unfair trade rules of GATT/ WTO which allow Monsanto to monopolize seed, five grain traders to monopolize trade, five processors to appropriate the value from producers, leaving farmers with not enough even to cover the cost of production and the cost of living. We stopped the WTO ministerial conferences in Seattle and Cancun. For Cancun, we prepared a report on the incomes lost by Indian farmers because of unfair free trade. In our assessment, Indian producers were losing $25 billion annually because of falling prices.

And in the spice gardens where I am visiting farmers, dumping linked to 'free trade' has dropped the price of the areca nut from 150 rupees to just 35 rupees. When zero-duty imports of soy oil were imposed on India through a WTO dispute, the price of one coconut fell from 10 rupees to 2 rupees, forcing farmers in Kerala, the land of the coconut, to chop down their coconut trees.

The false 'cheap' that is becoming the dominant measure of trade is created by the destruction of nature, of local economies, of farmers' livelihoods and freedom of people. 'Cheap' hides the externalities of injustice and exploitation, of non-sustainability and the violation of human rights.

This is why we need authentically fair trade, not the pseudo-Fairtrade that mimics the exploitative tendencies of unfair trade.

At Navdanya, the movement of seed savers and organic farmers in India, we define fairness as fairness to the Earth, fairness to producers (including producers in importing countries to avoid dumping) and fairness to consumers.

We have to change the rules of 'free trade' which define freedom for corporations and hide the new slavery of people. How can trade be free if it allows Monsanto to write the rules of intellectual property to monopolize the seed and rob farmers of their freedom to save and exchange seed? How can trade be free if it allows Cargill to write the rules of agriculture, destroying the livelihoods and lives of farmers, replacing our rich biodiversity and cultural diversity with a handful of 'cheap' commodities?

We need to put justice, dignity and people's freedom into the trade equation – and this is what Sally Blundell's excellent guide helps us do.

Vandana Shiva
Delhi

CONTENTS

Introduction

THE HISTORY OF the world is the history of... love? Conquest? Humanity, say some. The privileged few, say others. No. The history of the world is the history of trade. Driven by need, greed or curiosity, trade has inspired exploration, communication, discovery and enlightenment. It has given us book-keeping, navigational charts, maritime insurance, the clock. Even writing has been traced back to a basic form of accounting developed by Mesopotamian farming communities around 7000BCE to keep track of produce and exchanges. But the history of trade has shown it to be neither fair nor free. Its heavy-booted footprint has also left a trail of war, disease, land confiscation, colonization, environmental degradation and enslavement. Today, in a global environment in which countries are 'economies' and transnational companies have as many, if not more, rights than nation states, the fair trade movement has succeeded in providing an alternative to a system of trade that has disempowered farmers and producers throughout the Majority World.

Born, in recent times at least, out of a series of car boot/trunk sales in Kansas, fair trade grew out of a small number of Christian charitable groups undertaking direct-purchase projects in poor communities. From these humble beginnings it has grown into a hybrid creature sporting a profusion of different-colored labels, marks and seals across the globe. Depending on whom you talk to and which survey you read, fair trade is a social-justice movement, a tool for international development or an alternative market model that facilitates access for small-scale farmer co-operatives and worker collectives on terms that enable them to move from poverty to economic self-sufficiency. This it does by entering into long-term trading relationships that take into account the specific challenges of producer groups; by providing artisans and farmers, particularly those in the volatile commodities market, with guaranteed prices that cover the cost of production; by supporting initiatives identified by those groups to improve output, incomes and living standards.

The idea was quick to catch on. By the early 1960s a number of non-governmental organizations (NGOs) in Asia, Africa and Latin America were helping groups of local farmers and artisans sell their goods through like-minded development organizations in the US, the UK and Europe.

In some ways the success of fair trade belies business sense. A pro-poor program, based on the anti-commercial logic of buy high, sell low, should not be sailing through recessions and climatic catastrophes as it does. But sales continue to grow. In 2011 tens of millions of consumers in over 120 countries spent around $6.6 billion on Fairtrade-certified goods, an increase of 12 per cent over 2010. As US sociologists Laura Raynolds and Douglas Murray write: 'Mainstream economists would have us believe that consumers seek out the lowest price for goods of any given quality, maximizing their individual gains. But how then do we explain why millions of consumers around the world are now choosing certified Fair Trade products instead of other often cheaper options? Are they actively "voting with their money" for a different model of global trade that is tangibly "fairer" than conventional trade?'[1] Clearly yes. The fair trade movement operates alongside the organics movement in food, the anti-sweatshop movement in clothes and eco-labeling in timber as an initiative working specifically towards a more sustainable and socially just future than that offered by present-day processes of international trade and corporate expansion.

Fair trade today operates mainly through two channels: the World Fair Trade Organization (WFTO), a global network of 100-per-cent fair trade organizations that meet specific standards related to working conditions, wages, child labor, the environment and non-discrimination; and Fairtrade International, a certification body that identifies, through the Fairtrade label, mainly food items (including tea, coffee, wine, cocoa, honey, nuts, bananas, cotton, dried fruit, fresh fruit and vegetables, juices, quinoa, rice, spices and sugar) produced and traded in line with certain social and environmental criteria.

But the growth of the movement has brought with it a distinct set of challenges related to the nature and direction of fair trade. Is it a pro-poor, producer-focused alternative to conventional trade? Or is it a system of production and sales working within conventional trade to spread the benefits of fair trade as widely – some would say as thinly – as possible? Originally applied to small agricultural co-operatives, the Fairtrade label is now carried by specific product lines of big-name brands, including Nestlé, Starbucks and Kraft, even though the bulk of products sold by these corporations is conventionally produced and traded.

Some argue that any growth in the Fairtrade 'brand' has a positive spin-off for farmers in Majority World countries. 'If thousands more producers are to participate (in Fairtrade),' wrote Harriet Lamb, then director of the UK's Fairtrade Foundation, 'it needs the big boys to step up to the plate.'[2] Others are concerned that democratically run smallholder farmers will be pushed out of the Fairtrade loop as they find themselves incapable of meeting the demands of large corporations that are reluctant to spend time checking isolated farms at the far end of the supply chain – especially when a fully functioning Fairtrade-certified plantation is able to meet their requirements with minimal disruption to their working model. As Albert Tucker, former director of fair trade company

Twin Trading, argued, 'The fair trade mark should be regarded as a "badge of honor" not just a brand of food that demonstrates you are paying a little more to desperate farmers.'[3]

In 2011 Fair Trade USA (formerly TransFair USA) resigned its membership from Fairtrade International in preparation for its new initiative, Fair Trade For All. To implement the goal implicit in the name of this initiative it aims to expand fair trade certification to include more plantations and factories. It has also developed its own fair trade weighting for individual products by which only 25 per cent of the ingredients needs to be certified as fairly traded. Such moves are clearly aimed at increasing the volume of certified goods on the supermarket shelves, so bringing more farmers into the ambit of fair trade. Or so the argument goes. But the focus on quantity of sales over quality of trading relationship risks further marginalizing those that the alternative trade movement was established to support – small farmers unable to compete with large, plantation-based operations.

Is this fair trade lite? Or the demise of fair trade? As Rink Dickinson, co-founder and co-president of Equal Exchange in the US, said in a speech to the InterReligious Task Force on Central America in 2011, the gravest threat 'is the ongoing lowering of fair trade standards to the point where real fair trade groups cannot compete in the market because fair trade in name is cheap and well connected with the market

---

'Fairtrade' and 'fair trade'

Throughout this book, a distinction is drawn between 'Fairtrade' and 'fair trade'. The former refers to a certification label used for goods that have met criteria determined by Fairtrade International and FLO-CERT. The latter refers to the alternative trade movement as a whole, including those organizations operating under the ambit of the World Fair Trade Organization.

and access is actually worse than it was before this movement started in earnest in the Eighties'.[4]

The solution may lie in a new standard aimed at identifying goods traded by 100-per-cent fair trade organizations. Or it may lie in new initiatives such as the Organic Consumers Association's Fair World Project, aimed specifically to 'protect the term "fair trade" from dilution and misuse for mere PR purposes'.[5] Or it may lie in a bevy of new producer-owned labels. In November 2010, at the 4th General Assembly of the Latin America and Caribbean Network of Small Fair Trade Producers (CLAC), representatives launched the Small Producers Symbol, 'to give an identity to organized small producers in the market, in a world dominated by the big companies, where it is necessary to differentiate the small producer and their values'.[6]

In this book I begin by offering a brief overview of the history of trade and the political and economic processes brought to bear on this most ancient of practices. Chapter 2 looks at the rise of the fair trade movement from a series of car boot/trunk sales and imported cuckoo clocks in the US to a global movement shifting billions of dollars of crafts and commodities around the globe on behalf of marginalized farmers and artisans. Chapter 3 covers the rise and rise of neoliberal economic policies that have locked many Majority World countries into a wheel-spinning lack of progress and have given added impetus to the alternative trade movement. Chapter 4 looks at the evidence to date on whether fair trade is actually working. A relative latecomer to the goals of fair trade, environmental protection, discussed in Chapter 5, has now become one of the most important goals of fair trade. But all will come to naught if current moves to extend fair trade certification to transnational corporations continue to dilute fair trade standards. This will be discussed in Chapter 6 before a brief conclusion looks at the future of fair (alternative, ethical) trade as it works to differentiate an authentic movement working on behalf of the world's small farmers and artisans from its pretenders.

Sally Blundell
Christchurch, 2013

1 Laura T Raynolds and Douglas L Murray, 'The Fair Trade Future', *Policy Innovations*, The Carnegie Council, New York, 31 Jan 2008. **2** Harriet Lamb, 'Scale without Compromise', in John Bowes (ed), *The Fair Trade Revolution*, Pluto Books, New York, 2011. **3** Quoted in Jess Worth, 'Buy now, pay later', *New Internationalist*, 395, Nov 2006. **4** smallfarmersbigchange.coop/2011 **5** Dana Geffner, director Fair World Project, fairworldproject.org **6** fairworld-project.org

1 A short history of trade

Trade through the centuries, from the Italian city states and Marco Polo to the scramble for spices and the market for slaves. How the imperial trading companies lay the groundwork for an unequal world order – and how the idea of 'free trade' embraced by the British Victorians again becomes the dominant economic idea towards the end of the 20th century.

AT ITS MOST BASIC, trade – from the old Germanic word meaning 'track' or 'tread' – is a means of survival. Barter, the age-old exchange of commodities or services between reciprocal traders, put food into bellies, roofs over heads, clothes on backs. Even today, barter accounts for an estimated 25-30 per cent of all transactions worldwide.

The emergence of cities between 4000 and 3000BCE inspired a huge leap forward in trade and more sophisticated accounting systems as supply chains grew longer and units of currency replaced livestock and crops as a form of foreign exchange. The economic growth of Europe around the year 1000 followed the development of major commercial routes along the Mediterranean coast. From the 10th to the 13th centuries the city republics of northern Italy – Pisa, Venice, Florence and Genoa – grew into major trading centers where the merchant was king and the marketplace the thriving hub of commerce. A military pact with the Byzantine Empire in the 11th century granted Venetians tax-free travel throughout the Byzantine empire west of Constantinople, so allowing for the eventual expansion of a trading empire stretching from Greenland in the north to Peking in the east. Participation in the Crusades gave further impetus to these maritime republics as they forged new trade routes between east and west and the wealth of the new merchant class flourished.

By this time European demand for silks and spices from Asia was soaring. In 1254 Marco Polo accompanied his father Nikola on a journey from Constantinople across the Black Sea to the Crimea. Two years later he traveled to the Persian Gulf, through Iran and on to the Gobi Desert and China, opening up new trade routes to the Orient and further positioning Venice as a major port.

By the 15th century, marketplaces in Constantinople, Cairo, Alexandria, Damascus and Tabriz were displaying: an exotic array of silks and spices; silver, copper, iron and tin from the mines of central and eastern Europe; furs from Russia, Siberia and Bulgaria; leather, wool, incense and slaves.

Taking to the seas

The expansion of the Ottoman Empire and the fall of Constantinople in 1453 blocked the Silk Road and the overland spice-trade routes, so forcing Europe's traders to take to the seas in their quest for Asia's bounty of gold, silver and spices. To quell any dissent, a line

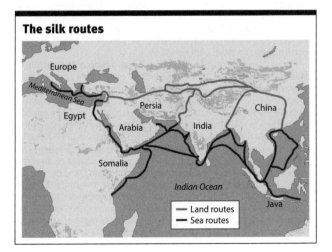

The silk routes

— Land routes
— Sea routes

was drawn across the map giving Spain the right to conquer non-Christian lands to the west of the Cape Verde Islands, and Portugal the right to take pagan countries to the east of the islands. In 1492 Christopher Columbus famously set sail for India. Westwards he went, hitting the Bahamas and what is now Haiti and the Dominican Republic in the Caribbean (hence the stubborn misnomer, the West Indies), finally making landfall in Venezuela on his third voyage in 1498. Twenty years later Hernan Cortés planted his legendary foot on Mexico. A further 14 years and

The story of spice

Clove, nutmeg, mace, cinnamon, pepper – an incantation of spices desired in Europe's marketplaces and the homes of the well-to-do as taste enhancers, food preservatives, medicines and a sure sign of wealth and social status. For centuries, caravans of up to 4,000 camels carried spices across ancient trails through the deserts of southern Asia and the Middle East to markets in the West. It took the battering force of the Crusades not only to reclaim Jerusalem but also to expel the Moors from Spain and so establish European control of the spice trade. But where did these spices grow? Spain and Portugal launched the search. Columbus sailed west, stumbling across a continent instead of the source of spices (in a bold act of wishful thinking he called the local chilis 'peppers', a confusion that lasts to this day). Portugal sent its ships eastward to Africa, from which they returned laden with gold, ostrich eggs and slaves. But no spices.

Finally, in early 1498, Vasco da Gama reached the island of Madagascar, where he found a guide to take him to the port of Calicut in southwestern India. There he found cinnamon (and some convertible souls) but little else. It was not until the middle of the 16th century that the Portuguese reached the Moluccas, the famed Spice Islands, where they promptly cowed the sultan of Malacca into granting them trading rights: 'Whoever is lord of Malacca,' observed Tomé Pires, its first Portuguese governor, in his book *Suma Oriental* (1512-15), 'has his hands on the throat of Venice.' But Portugal was unable to meet the growing demand for pepper, pepper prices were rising, and the country was aligned with the Spanish crown with which the Dutch Republic was at war. Dutch merchant and sailor Jan Huyghen van Linschoten had first-hand knowledge of the 'secret' spice trade routes used by the Portuguese, who inevitably lost their monopoly to the Netherlands. By the early 1600s the Dutch East India Company was the dominant force

Francisco Pizarro arrived in South America, eventually destroying the powerbase (and most of the population) of the Inca. In the meantime European exploration and settlement of the west coast of Africa was in full force. Many of these early explorations were led by the Portuguese: Bartolomeu Dias rounded the Cape of Good Hope in 1488, while the brutal and piratical Vasco da Gama established an all-water route around Africa to India in 1498. In the centuries to follow, the great nations of Europe – Portugal, Spain, the Netherlands, Britain – all took on leading roles in

in the Asian spice trade.

To keep international market prices high, spice production was deliberately limited. Almost the entire population of the Banda Islands, the source of nutmeg, was killed and replaced with European employees and slave labor in the fields. According to novelist Pramoedya Ananta Toer, islanders were also dispatched to destroy competitors' nutmeg and clove estates.[1]

In the meantime England was keen to get its own slice of the spice action. On New Year's Eve in 1600, Queen Elizabeth I chartered a company of 218 merchants, giving it a monopoly of trade between England and the Far East. The English East India Company, now considered one of the historical forces behind the modern 'globalized' world, was a monopolistic, limited-liability state-backed trading body. Its defeat of the Portuguese off the coast of India in 1612 gave it trading concessions from the Mughal Empire, ensuring ready access to the rich stores of cotton, silk, indigo, saltpeter and spices from south India and a major administrative role in Bengal, the country's richest province, granted to the Company for 10 pounds a year. It quickly set about establishing trading posts in Masulipatam on the east coast of India (1611), on the west coast in Surat (1612), on the east coast again in Madras (now Chennai) in 1639, and on the Hooghly (one of the mouths of the Ganges) in 1690. By 1652 there were 23 English trading posts in India.

By the late 18th century America had become involved in the spice business, its fast new clipper ships quickly dominating world trade in allspice, pepper, and vanilla, and turning Salem, Massachusetts, into a major trading port. So much pepper was imported from Sumatra that the price of pepper dropped to less than three cents a pound – but not before the proceeds had lined the substantial coffers of Boston-born Englishman Elias Hasket Derby, the country's first millionaire, who later endowed his pepper-based riches to the new Yale University. ■

finding new trade routes to meet the growing demand for precious metals, silk and spices.

England's command of the seas was similarly driven by the search for new trade routes and opportunities. By the time the spice trade was open to one and all, with profits no longer the enticement they were, the East India Company had turned its attention to England's apparently insatiable appetite for steeped *Camellia sinensis* – tea. By the 1790s, the Company was shipping 23 million pounds of Chinese tea leaves into London, accounting for more than 60 per cent of the total trade from Canton (now Guangzhou). There was a problem. China was not interested in any British imports; it wanted silver. To get silver, British traders hit upon the idea of opium – easy to transport, unlikely to spoil, easily grown in Bengal, then under British rule, and desired by the Chinese population (if not by the Chinese state). The East India Company

Slavery

Cheap raw materials brought huge profits to those further up the supply chain – the traders and merchants who monopolized the trade and the colonizing nations that filled their coffers with taxes. The next challenge was labor. As the colonies in the Americas grew, so did the need for a cheap workforce. After failed attempts to enslave Native Americans, the European settlers turned to Africa. Starting in the 1500s, half a century after Portuguese traders brought the first large cargo of slaves from West Africa to Europe, shiploads of Africans were transported to the American plantations in the profitable Triangle Trade that moved cloth, spirits, tobacco, beads and guns from Europe to Africa; slaves from Africa to the Americas; and cotton, sugar, molasses, tobacco and coffee (straight off slave-labor plantations) from the Americas back to Europe.

The whole deplorable system was responsible for the forced transportation and sale of an estimated 10-12 million Africans across the Atlantic. It took well over 350 years before Western countries began to heed calls to abolish the slave trade. In 1807, legislation on both sides of the Atlantic outlawed the importation of African slaves into the US and the transportation and importation of slaves by Britain and British colonies.

In 1948, the United Nations produced the Universal Declaration of

promptly assumed the monopoly of Bengalese opium-production and began smuggling the drug into China by the chest-load – 12,665 chests in 1828-29 – and offloading it at the rendezvous island of Lintin, where it was sold for cash paid into the Company's factory at Canton. Here merchants used the proceeds to buy silver, which was in turn used to buy tea and sold for great profit in London. In response to China's growing fury, the British superintendent of trade in Canton, Charles Elliot, persuaded the traders to surrender their stock of some 20,000 chests of opium on the understanding that they would be compensated by the British government, by then operating as the world's largest drug cartel. The Qing imperial authorities in China also insisted that British merchants sign bonds promising not to smuggle opium. Refusing to sign the bonds, Charles Elliot ordered the British community to withdraw from Canton and in 1839, in preparation

---

Human Rights, which includes the provision that 'No-one shall be held in slavery or servitude; slavery and the slave trade shall be prohibited in all their forms.' Problem solved? No. Recent estimates put the number of modern slaves at 27 million, about twice the estimated number of Africans sold into slavery during the years of the trans-Atlantic slave trade. Of these, 15-20 million are in or from South Asia and 50 per cent are children. In fields, factories, restaurants and mines, homes and armed services, their labor is present in the supply chains of such common items as cotton, tea, cocoa, sugar, rice, charcoal, carpets, clothing, toys, gems, tin, gold, bricks, fireworks and tantalum (mined in the Congo and sold for the manufacture of cellphones). They are the nameless faces building infrastructure in Burma, making toys in Chinese *laogai* prison camps, fighting wars in Sudan or working as prostitutes in Thailand, camel jockeys in the UAE or domestic servants in India.

The International Labour Organization (ILO) estimates the profits produced each year through the sale of humans to be $31.7 billion – more than that made in the illegal drug trade and soon to surpass global profits from the arms trade. The same report estimates that 12.3 million people are victims of forced labor worldwide, including more than 2.4 million as a result of human trafficking.[2] ∎

for war, Britain seized the island of Hong Kong. China lost the war and was forced to open its five ports to foreign merchants as well as to permit the territorial concession of Hong Kong to Britain for 150 years.

Systems of trade

During the 17th and 18th centuries the dominant economic philosophy was mercantilism, a simple export-or-die premise that aimed to restrict imports and boost exports in order to enrich colonial powers, fund increasingly powerful governments and expanding armies and feed growing and increasingly urbanized populations. To ensure such a 'favorable balance of trade', the state took on the job of prohibiting foreign goods, restricting commercial exchange with rival empires, subsidizing exports, restricting the export of precious metals (a pressing concern for those countries without mines) and creating monopolies among trading companies. One of the early exponents of mercantilism, 17th-century merchant Edward Misselden, pushed for the curtailment of the activities of the East India Company, claiming that the governmental concession allowing the Company to export large quantities of bullion put the country at risk of economic depression (Misselden later became a business associate of the East India Company – presumably he confined his attacks to late-night mutterings). In 1664, East India Company director Thomas Mun defended the organization, arguing that the 'ordinary means' to increase wealth and treasure 'is by Forraign Trade, wherein we must observe this rule; to sell more to strangers yearly than wee consume of theirs in value.'[3] Mun encouraged the purchase of materials at their source of supply rather than through intermediaries and pushed for the removal of taxes on imports of raw materials used in manufacturing exports.

Enter Adam Smith (1723-1790), the much-touted father of modern economics who tore mercantilist theories apart with his bold new concept of absolute advantage. It was impossible, he argued, for all nations to become rich at the same time following the laws of mercantilism. Smith insisted that government and economics were two separate realms – and that they should remain so. Prices should be determined by the laws of supply and demand and, left to themselves, self-interest, competition and free markets would cohere into a single recipe for the common good. An example: if the United States produced only wheat and the UK produced only cloth they would both benefit from unrestricted trade in wheat and cloth. This startlingly simplistic notion was later reshaped to the more dynamic concept of comparative advantage proffered by 19th-century English economist David Ricardo (Ricardo has taken the historical spotlight from Jane Marcet, an innovative thinker and academic who, in *Conversations on Political Economy* [1816] presented an eloquent summary of comparative advantage). This theory moved the focus from the absolute values of labor productivity to labor productivity ratios. Back to the US, while it may be a good producer of cloth it may be even better – meaning more profitable – at producing sugar, whereas Italy has great difficulty in producing sugar but is OK at producing cloth – not as good as the US but still OK. Under comparative advantage it makes more sense for the US to buy cloth from Italy and Italy to buy sugar from the US.

But advantage is a moveable feast. Problems arose as international trade rules became increasingly mired in a one-way transfer of wealth from relatively poor countries to relatively rich countries, and when all countries wanted to benefit from production further up the chain. In the years that followed, the trade pendulum increasingly favored *laissez-faire* capitalism, or the notion of free trade, as the dominant economic theory in the Western world.

A short history of trade

In 1846 Britain repealed its Corn Laws – ancient rules governing the import and export of grain to protect local farmers – so marking the abandonment of mercantilism and the beginning of the age of British free trade, or as near as it will get. The hugely contentious move resulted in a general decline of protectionism. By 1892, imports of wheat and flour by Britain had grown to nearly 10 times their volume in 1846. As grain prices fell, English landowners moved out of agricultural production. The burgeoning US agriculture sector took up the slack and Britain, no longer self-sufficient in food, moved towards manufactured goods for export in which it had a comparative advantage thanks to its ready access to capital endowment and technical superiority.

The spread of this new economic order, built on the pillars of free trade – *laissez faire*, the free mobility of capital and labor, and international property rights – relied on the assumption that markets produced economically efficient and ethically acceptable outcomes. By the 20th century, however, the social and political toll of uncontrolled market imperatives was all too apparent. Emerging out of the coal smoke of the Industrial Revolution was the reality of the largely unregulated factory system. Wages were punishingly low, hours long (12-16 a day), working conditions miserable. Under England's notorious Combination Acts, trade unions were banned and strikes outlawed. Although 1819 legislation prevented children eight and under from working in cotton mills (to the outrage of local capitalist interests), in non-textile industries children as young as five continued to be employed. In a speech in 1885 British cabinet member Joseph Chamberlain advocated a greater role for government within the industrial sector, claiming that, 'Government is the only organization of the whole people for the benefit of all its members... The community may and ought to provide for all its members benefits which it is impossible for individuals to provide by their solitary and separate efforts.'[4]

Alternative economic theories, most notably the interventionist views of British economist John Maynard Keynes (1883-1946), challenged the excesses of unbridled capitalism. Keynes argued for a more prominent role for government – particularly in times of recession – to restore equilibrium and full employment through systems of tariffs, international cartels and state trading. Keynes' theories, developed in the midst of the Depression of the 1930s, were seen as a necessary mechanism to roll back imperialism, stop the spread of communism and help so-called 'underdeveloped' nations to become prosperous economies. Beginning in the late 1940s, however, there emerged a new wave of free-market adherents. Through a series of thinktanks, this movement grew into a well-funded platform espousing a much-reduced role for government within the economy. Riding on the argument that protectionism had increased the severity of the Depression, what has come to be called the Liberal International Economic Order (version two, if you count Britain's free-market economic order of the 19th century) grew into an international logging operation clear-felling any barriers to the free flow of trade and capital.

The following decades saw a progressive shift of power from public to private interests as world trade rules and preferential trading arrangements backed a global regime aimed at minimizing impediments to the movement of capital and goods. The mantra of free trade has been taken so far as to challenge the right of sovereign governments to regulate labor conditions – in 1996 the World Trade Organization Singapore Ministerial Conference resulted in a declaration stating that the ministers 'reject the use of labor standards for protectionist purposes, and agree that the comparative advantage of countries, particularly low-wage developing countries, must in no way be put into question'.[5] Measures to protect the environment have been sacrificed for massive agricultural 'investments' and traditional knowledge has been hauled into the ambit of intellectual property laws.

And for whose benefit? While global poverty figures have dropped over the last 30 years, more than 80 per cent of the world's population lives in countries where income differentials are widening. The poorest 40 per cent of the world's population accounts for just 5 per cent of global income, while the richest 20 per cent accounts for three-quarters of world income. According to Oxfam, 97 per cent of the income generated by international trade benefits the nations that are rich or have a middle income. The global commodities market has pushed down prices (or kept them swinging erratically between low and lower) and forced small farmers in some of the world's poorest countries to compete with often heavily subsidized farmers from some of the world's wealthiest nations. The need for an alternative to free trade could not have been more clear.

1 Pramoedya Ananta Toer, 'The Book That Killed Colonialism', *New York Times*, 18 Apr 1999. 2 ILO, *A global alliance against forced labour*, Report of the Director-General, 2005. 3 nin.tl/13TTKxq 4 Quoted in Bruce Smith, *A Protest Against the Growing Tendency Toward Undue Interference by the State, with Individual Liberty, Private Enterprise, and the Rights of Property*, 1887, books. google.co.nz 5 Laura T Raynolds and Douglas L Murray, *op. cit.* 'The Fair Trade Future', *Policy Innovations*, The Carnegie Council, New York, 31 Jan 2008.

2 The revolution that went to market

The rise and rise of fair trade. A Kansas woman's solidarity initiative mushrooms into what is now the Ten Thousand Villages network of stores. Help for European refugees turns into major alternative trading operations in the cases of SERRV and Oxfam Trading. International organizations arise to establish standards and oversee fair trade labeling – and the pie becomes so big that transnationals want a piece of the action.

IT SEEMED A simple enough plan – to persuade buyers in the wealthier cities of the Global North to support small business initiatives on the other side of the economic divide. Developed in the middle of the last century, often by religious groups working in small, often remote communities across the Global South, the fledgling fair trade movement was a grassroots, development-based alternative to top-down, Western-led 'solutions' to poverty in poorer countries. The movement promptly set about developing markets through like-minded organizations, first for handcrafts and then for food items made or grown by artisans and farmers trying to make a sustainable living in the face of falling agricultural returns, geographic isolation, unemployment and social, religious, political or gender-based marginalization. It was goodwill selling, pro-poor, not-for-profit, ad hoc in its development and wildly committed to the cause.

Fair trade – which can also be termed 'alternative', 'ethical', 'solidarity' or 'direct' trade – is not new. In the late 1700s, abolitionists and Quaker societies launched a campaign against slave-made produce. Inspired by a series of pamphlets and posters, British consumers began a mass boycott against slave-grown sugar.

The revolution that went to market

Over just a few months, grocers reported that sugar sales had dropped by over a third while the sale of slave-free sugar from India increased tenfold. In 1792 James Wright, a Quaker and merchant of Haverhill, Suffolk, used an advertisement in the General Evening Post to declare:

'Being Impressed with a sense of the unparalleled SUFFERINGS of our FELLOW-CREATURES, the AFRICAN SLAVES in the WEST-INDIA ISLANDS, and also with the abominable Means practised in procuring them … and also with an Apprehension, that while I am Dealer in that Article, which appears to be a principal Support of the Slave Trade, I am encouraging Slavery, I take this Method of informing my Customers, that I mean to discontinue selling the Article of SUGAR (when I have disposed of the Stock I have on Hand), till I can procure it through Channels less contaminated, more unconnected with Slavery, and less polluted with Human Blood......'[1]

Half a century later a group of cloggers, shoemakers, joiners and weavers formed the Rochdale Equitable Pioneers Society in a collaborative bid to access basic goods though a system of trade (the 'Rochdale Method') based on honesty, transparency, fair prices and democratic representation, sowing the seeds of the modern co-operative movement and Britain's Co-operative Retail Trading Group (the Co-op).

The origins of the fair trade movement as it is today can be traced to Kansas businesswoman and Mennonite Central Committee (MCC) volunteer Edna Ruth Byler. In 1946 Byler traveled to Puerto Rico, a country still reeling from the Depression, a punishing hurricane and the closure of two-thirds of the island's textile factories. There she met women struggling to sell their finely stitched linen goods made through an MCC-run sewing class. The more affluent residents of Kansas, she thought, could provide a potentially long-term market, so giving a level of financial security to the Puerto Rican craftswomen while also giving her compatriots an insight into the Caribbean world on their doorstep. Over the following years Byler rallied together friends and fellow church members to build a market for these hand-sewn goods, beginning with a series of car boot/trunk sales and eventually taking a range of samples to a Mennonite conference in Switzerland. The linen textiles were saleable items, the designs were 'exotic', the story engaging and, in shoring up a market in the US and Canada, Byler saw a way to provide sustainable economic opportunities for artisans in Puerto Rico and, as her enterprise grew, Palestinian refugees in Jordan and wood carvers in Haiti.

Around the same time, in 1949, the Church of the Brethren in New Windsor, Maryland, launched a program to help refugees in post-war Europe establish an economic footing through the manufacture and sale of household items. Beginning with imported wooden cuckoo clocks from Germany, SERRV (Sales Exchange for Refugee Rehabilitation and Vocation) quickly expanded its range to include crafts made by artisans from Bangladesh, Thailand, Hong Kong and 'the Holy Land' and sold through a growing number of international gift shops and mail-order catalogues 'in a just and direct manner'.

Both organizations flourished. In the 1970s, Byler's project moved out of her basement to become Selfhelp Crafts of the World, still operating under the auspices of the MCC. In 1996 it morphed into Ten Thousand Villages, a retail company now with more than 100 stores in the US and Canada (the name is taken from a quote by Mahatma Gandhi: 'India is not to be found in its few cities but in the 700,000 villages'). By the time SERRV split from the Church of the Brethren in 1999, its sales had reached $5.5 million.

Similar projects were being developed in Britain. By the late 1950s, Oxfam UK (set up in 1942 as the

The revolution that went to market

Quaker-led Oxford Committee for Famine Relief to send supplies to women and children in enemy-occupied Greece during World War Two) was using its existing chain of shops to sell crafts made by Eastern European refugees and, later, by Chinese refugees in Hong Kong. In 1964 it registered Oxfam Activities Ltd, with a subsidiary, Oxfam Trading, which is often described as the first alternative trading organization. The following year it launched its Helping-by-Selling scheme and in 1975 it established its Bridge program to provide small-scale producers with technical training and funding and a fair price for crafts sold through a network of volunteer-run charity shops.

Parallel initiatives were taking place in the Netherlands. In 1959, the Dutch importing organization SOS ('Support for Underdeveloped Regions', later known as SOS Wereldhandel and now as Fair Trade Organisatie) was founded by a group of young Catholic activists in the town of Kerkrade. After an initial venture, supplying milk powder to malnourished children in Sicily, in 1967 it launched a trading program beginning with wooden ware from Haiti, plant hangers and bamboo ashtrays from the Philippines, earthenware from Mexico and leather sandals from a Dalit community in India sold through exhibitions and mail-order catalogues. It aligned itself with the network of Third World Groups, which had been established by the solidarity group Sugar Cane Action in protest against the excess production of sugar in EEC countries (its slogan: 'By buying cane sugar you give people in poor countries a place in the sun of prosperity'). The Third World Groups developed into a chain of retail stores known as World Shops. As SOS Wereldhandel established subsidiary organizations in Germany, Austria, Switzerland and Belgium, the network of World Shops spread across Europe and in 1974 the National Association of World Shops was founded.

Shoulder to shoulder

The early stirrings of alternative trade grew out of the desire of usually faith-based initiatives to support refugees and impoverished communities by selling their crafts through church-run stalls and mail-order catalogues. The World Shop network, however, was a vehicle for a growing solidarity movement supporting politically and economically marginalized peoples across the globe. In 1973, World Shops were involved in the successful boycott of coffee imports from Angola in protest against the colonial war in that country and to deny the Portuguese colonial regime the profits from coffee sales. Six years later, solidarity movements around the world threw their support behind coffee co-operatives in Nicaragua in support of that country's Sandinista government and in defiance of an embargo imposed by the Reagan administration. In the US, the fledgling Equal Exchange organization used a fiercely protected legal loophole that defined coffee's origin by the country where it was roasted rather than where it was harvested (it was imported from Dutch ATO, Stichting Ideele) to sell Nicaraguan coffee through an informal chain of natural food stores and consumer co-operatives.

At the same time products from southern African frontline states were sought for their anti-apartheid associations. So too was coffee from Mexico, Argentina and Brazil, where the revolutionary liberation-theology movement was seeking a renewed focus on the poor, so radicalizing a church increasingly allied to the working classes and concentrating not on the rewards of heaven but the here and now of political and economic struggle. In Britain, TWIN (Third World Information Network), formed in 1985 with the support of the Greater London Council, launched its career by selling cigars from Cuba and rocking chairs from Nicaragua. Today it works with over 50 democratic farmer organizations in 18 countries to secure access to international markets and develop new business opportunities and models. The phrase 'fair trade' was reportedly first used in its current context by the founding chair of Twin Trading, Michael Barratt Brown, during a Trade and Technology Conference in London in 1985: 'There is too much unfair trade in the world today. Let's have more Fair Trade.'

Central to the development of this alternative trade movement was the growing debate over poverty and aid. Already the UN and the European Community had devised compensatory finance schemes either to recompense poor producers if market prices for their goods fell below agreed levels or to subsidize commodity producers in former European colonies. In 1968, moreover, the United Nations Conference on Trade and Development (UNCTAD) had agreed that 'trade not aid' was the best method of development assistance.

At the same time the grand plans and big promises of traditional systems of aid were increasingly seen as top-down and patronizing, and their one-size-fits-all think-big projects were being shown to be far removed from the needs and reality of the world's poor. A prime example was the Food and Nutrition Policy and Planning Strategy of the 1970s supported by the World Bank and USAID, which aimed at converting 'illiterate peasants' into cheap labor for transnational capital. Such a system, argued Colombian anthropologist Arturo Escobar, was a form of neo-imperialism mired in a post-World War Two mindset that saw industrialization and international competition as the building blocks for the 'development' of otherwise 'backward economies'. As Escobar wrote, 'Development has become the grand strategy through which the transformation of the not-yet-too-rational Latin American/Third World subjectivity is to be achieved.'[2]

Bogged down in Western-defined indicators and

goals, aid programs appeared to be faltering under a system dogged by lack of accountability and recipient feedback while failing to reach those most in need. Increasingly, too, aid was being implicated in a raft of economic changes imposed on the countries of the Global South by the world's international financial institutions. As Yash Tandon, executive director of intergovernmental thinktank The South Centre, argues, rather than mitigating poverty, aid is 'an added arsenal in the armory of the industrialized countries to get the developing countries to conform to their policies, and these policies have not been development friendly'.[3]

But the political will to develop a stronger price foundation for commodity farmers in the Global South and to uncouple aid from the new and largely untested ideology of free trade was lacking. In its absence, development agencies and solidarity groups – with backing from trades unions, the women's movement, environmental and anti-nuclear groups – took up the

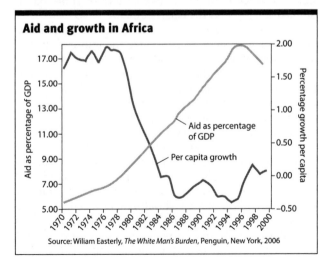

Aid and growth in Africa

Source: Wiliam Easterly, *The White Man's Burden*, Penguin, New York, 2006

The artisans of old Delhi

Delhi, 1966. Academic turned social activist Dr Shyam Sharma comes to a startling conclusion. The solution to the rampant poverty he saw around him was not to be found in aid, but in trade. It was trade, he realized, that would bring long-term development and address the health, educational and vocational needs of underprivileged people in an urban area marked by poverty, joblessness and hopelessness. In fair trade he saw the potential for income security, personal development and the dignity that results from the ability to feed, clothe and educate oneself and one's family. And in reaching out to marginalized groups he also recognized the capability of democratically run, locally based co-operatives and associations to challenge discrimination based on religion, caste and gender. He established Tara (Trade Alternative Reform Action) Projects, a fair trade organization offering training opportunities for the unemployed and those working in the poorly paid and highly exploitative jewelry and souvenir industries. Tara today, under the leadership of Sharma's daughter Moon Sharma, provides artisans with a living wage and access to savings and microcredit schemes, education for artisans' children (Tara is an outspoken critic of child labor) and environmental programs. ∎

slack to develop an alternative system of trade based on partnership and transparency.

Even in its earliest incarnations, the fair trade movement was quick to recognize the impossibility of direct trade with farmers and manufacturers scattered in often remote villages or urban slums throughout the Majority World. But in forming collectives and co-operatives these growers and artisans were not only able to negotiate with northern NGOs but could also enjoy increased solidarity and economies of scale.

The goal of these groups was not craft-making *per se* but the establishment of viable income-generating initiatives as an alternative to the poorly paid and insecure informal sector that characterized many of the countries in which development agencies were working. The scale of the underground economy is vast. Between 50 and 75 per cent of non-agricultural work in the countries of the Global South is found in the informal sector. Entry is easy, resources local and often free, and education requirements are minimal. Those involved are poor, often landless, and invariably marginalized on the basis of gender, caste, ethnicity and religion. Women, particularly single women, are disproportionately represented – according to Anvita Gupta *et al*, of the 94 per cent of Indian women engaged in the informal sector, nearly half are sole supporters of their families.[4]

Down on the farm

Handcrafts were an easy pitch. They were attractive, exotic (this at a time of often high import restrictions) and the stories struck at the consciences of rich-world consumers. But the introduction of food products – coffee, tea, sugar, rice – on to the shelves of World Shops was a clear politicization of the burgeoning alternative trade movement. It recognized the ongoing obstacles to smallholder farmers trying to gain market access: lack of capital, no sales outlets, rising prices of inputs such as seeds and fertilizers, poor communication systems, inadequate systems of quality control, the vicissitudes of weather, geographic isolation, changes in the availability of raw materials, lack of market information and limited access to affordable credit – not to mention a pricing system thrashed out in the remote commodity exchanges of London or New York.

While small-scale farmers dominate production of the world's most common agricultural commodities (70 per cent of the world's coffee, for example, is grown on small-scale family farms in Latin America, Asia and Africa), they capture only a low and declining share of the final purchase price. The major cost of a store-bought jar of coffee is taken by shippers and 'roasters', a euphemism for the giants of the coffee industry such as Nestlé and Kraft Foods. Another 1 per cent is taken by the exporters – the traders and

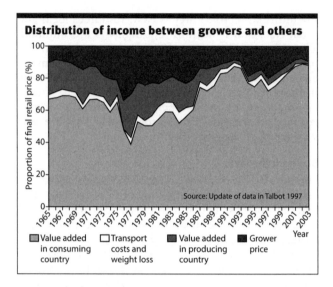

intermediaries who buy the coffee from the producers. Farmers, those who carry the greatest risk in terms of climatic conditions, crop health and fluctuating costs of farm inputs, are left with a pitiful share of 3-10 per cent, leaving them with no buffer to protect them from price fluctuations and natural disasters – let alone to fund farm upkeep and crop maintenance.

In recognition of the challenges facing small farmers – and the fact that many artisans were turning to craft to compensate for diminishing agricultural returns – the young alternative trade movement gravitated increasingly towards food items. Alternative trade organizations such as GEPA in Germany, Fair Trade Organizatie and Stichting Ideele in the Netherlands, Equal Exchange in the US and Twin Trading in Britain entered into trading partnerships with small-scale coffee co-operatives, searching out sympathetic roasters, distribution networks and stores to put their retail weight behind the small coffee farmers of the world.

It was not easy. To retain quality and value, the coffee co-operatives had to learn new processing techniques, step up quality control, negotiate the finer aspects of exporting, and often master new organic farming techniques. And they had to deal with all this without the massive economies of scale associated with large coffee plantations while also having to cope with the limitations of geographic isolation, lack of education, poor infrastructure and, always, lack of funds. As Rink Dickinson of Equal Exchange has said: 'Only mission-driven traders and nonprofits and visionary co-ops would take on this type of task... We were able to take advantage of that market, pay farmers well above market price, and find stores and consumers who cared about farmers and fairness as well as product quality.'

By the early 1970s, World Shops had appeared across Europe, shelves crammed with Tanzanian coffee and tea, Algerian orange juice and wine, Mozambican cashews, Cuban rum and Nicaraguan coffee. The craft-food ratio tilted, from 80-20 per cent of World Shop stocks in 1992 to 26-74 a decade later. As super-markets and large companies increased their share of Fairtrade-certified products (more about this in Chapter 5), the demand for fair trade food grew even further. Today, bananas, coffee, cocoa, sugar, tea, wine, fruit juices, nuts, spices and rice dominate fair trade sales statistics in the rich world. In addition to these food products, other non-food products have been added to the Fairtrade range, such as flowers and cotton.

Mexican beans

Until the late 1970s, the small coffee farmers of the Santa Maria and Guevea de Humboldt municipalities of the southwestern Mexican state of Oaxaca faced huge barriers to get their produce to market. Roads were almost non-existent, communication and public transport inadequate and housing, healthcare and education all poor. Already low coffee returns were further eroded by greedy intermediaries (or 'coyotes') and a drop in global coffee prices. The development of new logging roads in the 1970s provided new transport opportunities and in 1982 a group of farmers came together to share the production, marketing and distribution of locally produced coffee. With advice from a Dutch Jesuit mission team they formed the Unión de Comunidades Indígenas de la Región del Istmo (UCIRI) and began selling direct to Inmecafe, the Mexican Institute of Coffee. Resisting pressure from Inmecafe to increase agrochemical production – as part of the woefully misnamed 'green revolution' – they aligned themselves instead with an alternative export market offered by visiting Dutch and German solidarity groups that effectively bypassed the traditional street buyers and Inmecafe.

In 1985, UCIRI sent its first direct coffee export to Dutch specialty coffee importer Simon Lévelt and the German alternative trading organization GEPA. The success of UCIRI attracted more farmers and the co-operative began looking for new trading partners. In 1988, it approached Dutch development agency Solidaridad about developing a product label signifying fair trade criteria. This led to the establishment of the Max Havelaar Foundation and the world's first fair trade labeling initiative. The coffee was imported by Dutch company Van Weely, roasted then sold to World Shops and retailers across the Netherlands. In just two years UCIRI coffee sales in the Netherlands increased tenfold while UCIRI's membership grew to more than 2,000 farmers across 19 municipalities, all of them active in organic agriculture, and exporting to Belgium, Canada, Denmark, Finland, France, Germany, Holland, Ireland, Italy, Japan, Sweden, Switzerland and the US. Today, UCIRI continues to provide technical and financial assistance for the manufacture, storage, transportation and marketing of Fairtrade, organic coffee. It funds specific health, education and nutrition programs and lobbies for autonomous Indian rights and the preservation of indigenous languages and cultures.

A flurry of acronyms

Out of the scattering of church bazaars, World Shops, mail-order catalogues and food co-operatives, the alternative trade movement began to organize. Increasing sales success and the desire for more support and co-ordination amongst alternative trading organizations (ATOs) inspired the development of

---

An irritating tract

For DH Lawrence, it was a mere 'tract' written under an irritating pseudonym. According to novelist Pramoedya Ananta Toer, it was the book that 'killed colonialism'. *Max Havelaar*, the inspiration behind the Max Havelaar Foundation name, is an 1860 novel by Multatuli (Latin for 'I have suffered greatly'), the pen name of Eduard Douwes Dekker (1820-1887), a former employee of the Dutch East Indies government. The protagonist of the title is an idealistic Dutch colonial official based in Java who battles against the system of forced cultivation imposed on Indonesia's peasants. To increase diminishing revenue and assure investors of long-term property rights and a fixed supply of export crops, the Dutch colonial government was forcing Indonesian farmers to grow a quota of commercially tradable crops such as tea and coffee, instead of staple foods such as rice. It had also introduced a tax collection system by which farmers had to surrender a portion of their agricultural produce to the colonial power. The combination of these strategies caused widespread poverty and starvation, effectively turning Java, according to Pramoedya, into 'an agricultural sweatshop'.

The publication of *Max Havelaar: Or the Coffee Auctions of the Dutch Trading Company* shamed the Dutch government into creating a new ethical policy to promote irrigation, allow inter-island migration (peasants were previously forbidden by law to move away from their hometowns) and provide education to some (read loyalist) classes of natives. Pramoedya claims that *Max Havelaar*, since translated into 34 languages, was responsible for the nationalist movement that ended Dutch colonialism in Indonesia and which was instrumental in the call for decolonization in Africa and elsewhere in the world. ■

new umbrella bodies that have become critical players in the fair trade movement. In 1989 the International Federation of Alternative Traders (IFAT, now the World Fair Trade Organization) emerged as a global network of fair trade organizations aimed at strengthening their credibility in the eyes of political decision-makers, lending institutions, mainstream businesses and consumers and providing a forum for the exchange of information and ideas related to trade justice. It also set about developing a list of basic principles to be used as a benchmark for what was increasingly being referred to as 'fair trade'. According to former IFAT director Carol Wills: 'The word "fair" wasn't the word that was used at all to start with, it was "alternative"; that these types of organization were providing an alternative to conventional international trade which tended to marginalize small producers. I think alternative was rather a good word, because it was alternative in all kinds of ways: cutting out the middleman, trading directly; alternative distribution channels; alternative work force, volunteers in many cases... But then the word went out of fashion in a lot of countries and tended to get associated with brown rice and sandals and beards.'[5]

The following year, 1990, 11 of the oldest and largest ATOs from nine European countries came together to form the European Fair Trade Association (EFTA) and lobby for the wider procurement of fair trade products by public administrations. In 1994, the Network of European World Shops (NEWS!) was established to improve communication and collaboration among the 15 national World Shop associations. It also initiated European World Shops Day as a Europe-wide day-long fair trade campaign – now a global celebration run by the WFTO.

In 1997, European licensing initiatives created an international body, the Fairtrade Labelling Organizations International (FLO), based in Bonn, Germany, to homogenize standards and administer certification. This initiative brought together the Max Havelaar fair trade certification scheme and TransFair, a competitive seal that had started in Germany and which had begun importing plantation-grown tea on the grounds that it was impossible to procure tea from farmer-run smallholdings. The idea was anathema to the Dutch but, in forming FLO, the first steps towards certifying

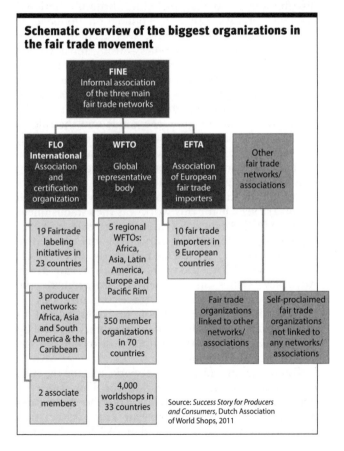

Schematic overview of the biggest organizations in the fair trade movement

FINE
Informal association of the three main fair trade networks

FLO International
Association and certification organization

WFTO
Global representative body

EFTA
Association of European fair trade importers

Other fair trade networks/ associations

19 Fairtrade labeling initiatives in 23 countries

5 regional WFTOs: Africa, Asia, Latin America, Europe and Pacific Rim

10 fair trade importers in 9 European countries

3 producer networks: Africa, Asia and South America & the Caribbean

350 member organizations in 70 countries

Fair trade organizations linked to other networks/ associations

Self-proclaimed fair trade organizations not linked to any networks/ associations

2 associate members

4,000 worldshops in 33 countries

Source: *Success Story for Producers and Consumers*, Dutch Association of World Shops, 2011

plantation-grown produce were taken. In 2004, FLO split into FLO-CERT, which inspects and certifies producer organizations and audits traders, and Fairtrade International, which is now responsible for setting international Fairtrade standards, for certifying production and auditing trade according to these standards, and for labeling products.

The increasing professionalization of fair trade distribution networks, including Britain's national labeling initiative Fairtrade Foundation (founded at the beginning of the 1990s), was accompanied by increasing attention to awareness-raising and advocacy work. Volunteers and the occasional paid staff member launched into research projects, campaign materials, public information events and promotions. Fair trade products were accompanied by information on the people who made or grew the goods and the role of the fair trade organization with which they worked, so creating a direct link between consumers in the Global North and the farmer or artisan groups trying to make a living in the rural regions or urban squats thousands of kilometers from the shop counter. An important vehicle for this work was the establishment of the FINE Advocacy Office in Brussels in 1998, supported, managed and funded by the alternative trade movement, represented then by FLO, IFAT, NEWS and EFTA. Today, FINE runs a Fair Trade Advocacy Office in Brussels to co-ordinate the advocacy activities of fair trade organizations in Europe, draw public attention to issues related to social justice and ecological sustainability and lobby individual governments and joint institutions on the importance of fair trade.

Today, regional fair trade networks include the Asia Fair Trade Forum, Cooperation for Fair Trade in Africa (COFTA), the Association Latino Americana de Commercio Justo and the Fair Trade Association of Australia and New Zealand (FTAANZ). National networks include Ecota Fair Trade Forum in Bangladesh, Fair Trade Group Nepal, Associated Partners for Fairer Trade Philippines, Fair Trade Forum India and the Kenya Federation for Alternative Trade (KEFAT).

Big umbrellas

Fair trade products are now traded and marketed through two distinct channels: the organizational route (through the WFTO) and the product certification route (via Fairtrade International).

Fairtrade International and WFTO share common principles. First, farmers and artisans must be organized into co-operatives or collectives. This not only cuts out the lengthy chain of intermediaries that typifies conventional trade (and cuts into the final price given to the producer) but also enables farmers and artisans to reduce raw material costs, share transport costs, access credit, pool resources in order to purchase new equipment or access technical advice and training,

---

Pinning it down

In 2001 FINE, representing the four main fair trade networks, agreed on the following definition of fair trade:

'Fair Trade is a trading partnership, based on dialogue, transparency and respect, that seeks greater equity in international trade. It contributes to sustainable development by offering better trading conditions to, and securing the rights of, marginalized producers and workers – especially in the South. Fair Trade organizations, backed by consumers, are engaged actively in supporting producers, awareness raising and in campaigning for changes in the rules and practice of conventional international trade.'

The goals of fair trade, as formulated with this definition, are to:

- deliberately work with marginalized producers and workers in order to help them move from a position of vulnerability to security and economic self-sufficiency;
- empower producers and workers as stakeholders in their own organizations;
- actively play a more substantial role in the global arena when it comes to achieving greater equity in international trade. ∎

and negotiate better terms and prices. Other baseline provisions include the payment of a fair or 'floor' price that covers the cost of production and represents a fair wage for producers; prepayment to avoid indebtedness; decent working conditions; environmental sustainability; the development of long-term trading relationships; and a commitment not to use child labor outside permissible 'light work' (defined by the ILO as non-hazardous work by 12-14 year olds for less than 14 hours a week).

A fair price

A minimal standard for fair trade and probably the most widely understood criterion is the payment of a fair and fairly negotiated price that covers the costs of sustainable production. According to FINE, a fair price is one that is 'mutually agreed between Fair Trade producers and buyers with the objective of providing a living wage and of covering the costs of sustainable production (all production costs are taken into account)'. While Fairtrade International's minimum price system is complex, as it includes variations for regional costs of living and product quality, it has been broadly broken down into cost of production + cost of living + cost of complying with Fair Trade standards. FLO standards also require the payment of a social premium to producers on top of the minimum price, which is directed toward community development projects chosen by co-operatives or disbursed to hired workers.

This was a sharp departure from the price system of the conventional market in which commodity prices changed daily in response to production amounts and weather conditions, while speculators amplified price shifts and brokers tried to drive the best bargain they could from producers. For craft products, fair trade pays the maximum amount that is feasible on the market. Because the production process in non-agricultural sectors is more complicated, it is difficult to provide such products with a certified label. Prices for handcrafts are negotiated between buyer and seller. These negotiations can be challenging, as Paul Myers of Ten Thousand Villages explains: 'It becomes sensitive at the point where we determine what's fair, and then we add on our costs, and then the price we need to charge for it at the end is too high. At that point we have to go back to the artisans and say, "We can't buy it because we can't sell it at that price".'[6] ∎

The WFTO 10 principles of fair trade

1 Creating opportunities for economically disadvantaged producers.
2 Transparency and accountability.
3 Fair trading practices, including prompt payments.
4 Payment of a fair price.
5 Ensuring no child labor and no forced labor.
6 Commitment to non-discrimination, gender equity and freedom of association.
7 Ensuring good working conditions.
8 Providing capacity building.
9 Promoting fair trade.
10 Respect for the environment.

But there are distinct differences between the two approaches. The WFTO mark is not a product label; rather, it identifies organizations that demonstrate a 100-per-cent commitment to fair trade in all their business activities and subscribe to the 10 WFTO principles (that said, at the time of writing, the WFTO has introduced plans to establish a product symbol identifying those goods made or imported by its member organizations). As of 2010 the WFTO had 472 member organizations and individuals in 74 countries.

Fairtrade International, meanwhile, sets standards for small-scale producer co-operatives, systems that use hired labor (like plantations), and buyers and traders. It defines both minimum standards (which must be met for inclusion in its fair trade registry) and progress standards, which set benchmarks for continual improvements in producer communities' production, governance, and business practices.

As a minimum requirement, producer organizations cannot discriminate against members or restrict new membership on the basis of 'race, color, sex, sexual orientation, disability, marital status, age, religion, political opinion, ethnicity or social origin'[7]. There must be transparent democratic governance (for co-operatives) and free association of workers and the right to collective bargaining (for plantations). Standards of occupational safety and sustainable production processes must be met and training in agriculture and business must be available. As well as the specified minimum price or the market price (whichever is the greater) buyers must provide pre-finance of up to 50 per cent of the expected value of the purchase if requested and pay an established fair trade premium to be used for community or business development projects as determined by the farmers' co-operative or a plantation's Joint Body.

For hired labor (workers on plantations, for example) organizations must safeguard workers' rights (including the right to join or form unions) and secure progress to better pay and conditions; they must constitute a Joint Body that includes elected worker representatives and management appointees. Working conditions must be equitable for all workers, organizations must pay salaries equal to or higher than legally established minimum wages, or the regional average for the sector.

Besides these common principles, FLO-CERT develops product standards for around 200 specific products, including minimum price and premium. In some cases, there are two documents per product (one for small-scale producers and another for hired labor). These figures exclude sales of most fair trade crafts and artisanal goods, for which formal standards have yet to be developed.

Fairtrade International also licences ATOs and mainstream businesses to use its certification label on their packaging and promotional materials to show that the product has met the requisite standards. It has also developed standards for 'composite' products in which at least 50 per cent of the total ingredients are sourced from fair trade producers. Fairtrade International also offers market information and technical

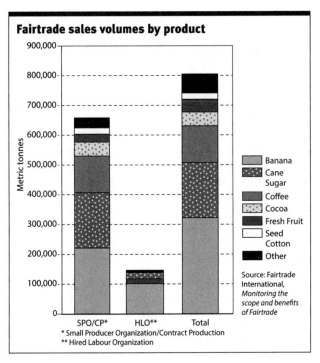

Fairtrade sales volumes by product

Metric tonnes

Banana
Cane Sugar
Coffee
Cocoa
Fresh Fruit
Seed Cotton
Other

Source: Fairtrade International, *Monitoring the scope and benefits of Fairtrade*

SPO/CP* HLO** Total

* Small Producer Organization/Contract Production
** Hired Labour Organization

capacity building services to producers through its Producer Business Unit and a network of liaison officers in developing countries.

Growing the market

In the early years of alternative trade it was all about the cause. People bought the Puerto Rican stitchcraft, the cuckoo clocks, the Haitian woodenware, even the coffee, because these were worthy causes that, let's be honest, didn't take a lot of effort. Quality? Not so important.

But this has changed as a result of increasing competition from mainstream for-profit retailers and a slew of new mail-order catalogs peddling 'ethnic' craft products – not to mention the move to higher-rent main street premises and the daily battle for customer consideration in supermarkets. As well as holding a candle for social justice, alternative trading organizations realized that, in order to survive, they had to strike a balance between the needs and capacities of suppliers on the one hand, and the demands and desires of consumers on the other.

To increase saleability and resolve quality issues, many ATOs began working more actively with producer groups, providing technical advice, training, design input and information related to tastes and trends in importing countries. This entrenched the notion and practice of partnership, further differentiating ATOs from conventional traders while encouraging a level of professionalization and responsiveness to consumer preferences in farmer and artisan collectives.

By the beginning of the 21st century the once eclectic mix of crafts and some coffee had grown into a comprehensive range of Fairtrade-certified coffee, chocolate and cocoa, fruit (pineapples, melons, mangoes), honey, nuts, spices, rice, wine, flowers and footballs.

Fairtrade schools, churches and towns began popping up across Europe – 500 in the UK alone. Brands such as Cafédirect and Divine chocolate, developed in partnership with producer organizations, became household names. In 2000, The Co-operative retail chain in the UK introduced its own-brand Fairtrade chocolate bar. In 2004, Tesco, Britain's largest retailer, introduced its range of Fairtrade products. As sales of Fairtrade-certified goods continued their upward curve and as large corporations tried to elbow in on the ethically minded consumer sector, plantation-made goods – tea, bananas, flowers – were progressively drawn into the fair trade sector. Spreading the benefits of fair trade, said some. Swimming with sharks, said others. As the likes of Nestlé, already under fire for marketing baby foods in poorer countries in contravention of World Health Organization guidelines, introduced their Fairtrade coffee lines, the murmurs of dissatisfaction became a roar.

1 abolition.e2bn.org/abolition_view **2** Arturo Escobar, 'Power and Visibility: Development and the Invention and Management of the Third World', *Cultural Anthropology*, 3:4, Oct 2009. **3** southcentre.org/index **4** Anvita Gupta, Dr Geetika, Tripti Singh, 'Women Working in Informal Sector in India: A Saga of Lopsided Utilization of Human Capital', ipedr.com/vol4/106-M00051 **5** Quoted in Alex Nicholls and Charlotte Opal, *Fair Trade: Market-Driven Ethical Consumption*. Sage Publications, London, 2004. **6** Quoted in Mary Ann Littrell and Marsha Ann Dickson, *Social Responsibility in the Global Market: Fair Trade of Cultural Products*, Thousand Oaks, CA, Sage Publications, 1999. **7** FLO 2009.

3 The problem with free trade

We would not need an alternative system of fair trade if the existing global trading structure was fit for purpose. But instead the dominant ideology of free trade has been imposed all over the world – except where it suits rich countries to retain their own subsidies. Small farmers and their families are paying a terrible price.

FOR THE FLEDGLING fair trade movement, equitable and transparent trade was a tool for development, a way to support and empower marginalized farmers and artisans as they developed a sustainable livelihood and a level of self-determination. Working on the edges of the marketplace these small, often volunteer-run, importing organizations worked to carve out a niche market for crafts and commodities procured in a manner that was transparently non-exploitative. The counterpoint to this fringe, largely consumer-driven movement, however, was the gathering tsunami of free-trade ideologies that came crashing down on small farmers and rural communities throughout the world towards the end of the 20th century.

The rise and rise of the neoliberal agenda grew out of the efforts to rebuild Europe after a global depression and the devastation of World War Two. The Monetary and Financial Conference at Bretton Woods, New Hampshire, in 1944, brought together 730 delegates from 44 allied nations with a simple goal: to establish a system of rules and procedures to govern monetary relations among independent nation-states and to develop new strategies to address the 'under-development' of 'Third World' countries. The job at hand, passed over to the newly formed World Bank (originally the International Bank for Reconstruction and Development) and the International Monetary

Fund (IMF), was to unlock the growth potential of low-productivity countries and help more 'advanced countries' to find overseas markets and investment opportunities (this at a time when US productivity had doubled during the war).

How to do this? The ideological manual included reducing barriers to the cross-border movement of goods, services, capital and, to a certain extent, of people and labor, and reducing state expenditure and industry support.

Three years after the Bretton Woods conference, 23 countries signed the new General Agreement in Trade and Tariffs, a set of rules aimed at reducing barriers to international trade through a series of 'rounds' (in 1994 its functions were taken over by the newly formed World Trade Organization). At the time of writing, the Doha Round, launched in 2001, remains snagged on a rock of unresolved issues related to agricultural subsidies.

The institutions involved in promoting such mechanisms were strongly biased towards the world's strongest nations, especially the US. Votes in the IMF are weighted according to member nations' financial contributions. Under this system, the US currently has 17.7 per cent of the vote while India, with more than three times the population, has 2.4 per cent. Because constitutional changes in the IMF require 85 per cent of the vote, the US has the right of veto. Across the World Bank Group, high-income countries have over 60 per cent of voting power; middle-income countries such as India, China and Brazil have around a third of votes while low-income countries languish on just 6 per cent.

The term 'Washington Consensus' was coined in 1989 to describe a set of policy prescriptions drafted by economist John Williamson and forming the basis of standard reform packages for impoverished Majority World countries. It was originally aimed at the very

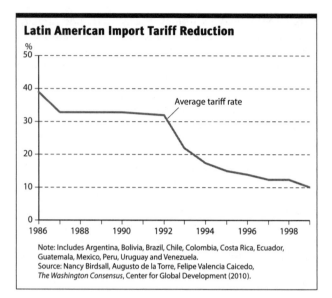

Latin American Import Tariff Reduction

Note: Includes Argentina, Bolivia, Brazil, Chile, Colombia, Costa Rica, Ecuador, Guatemala, Mexico, Peru, Uruguay and Venezuela.
Source: Nancy Birdsall, Augusto de la Torre, Felipe Valencia Caicedo, *The Washington Consensus*, Center for Global Development (2010).

real problems unfolding in Latin America in the 1980s, resulting from a sudden hike in the price of imported oil, mounting levels of external debt, soaring international interest rates and loss of access to additional foreign credit. In line with Washington Consensus policies Latin American countries were forced to cut government spending, reduce protectionism, increase exports, relax rules on trade and investment, and open domestic services to the market.

In contrast to prevailing views that underdevelopment required a proactive state aimed at expanding production for the domestic market – using a range of mechanisms such as import-substitution programs, state-owned firms and banks, the subsidizing of infant industries, price controls, high import tariffs and quotas – Latin American countries, reeling from the debt crisis, embarked on a deep and highly disruptive program of open competition, market orientation and state expenditure cuts. Import quotas were sliced and tariffs diced, the latter falling from nearly 50 per cent in the early 1980s to around 33 per cent in 1990 then down to 10 per cent in 1999. Restrictions on foreign investment were lifted, public banks and enterprises privatized (in Latin America more than 800 public enterprises were privatized between 1988 and 1997) and foreign banks encouraged to establish local presences.

As government intervention came to be seen as a distortion of the economy, and as state-led import-substitution gave way to a market-led model, Latin America's recently restored democracies stripped down the usual safety nets of schooling for the poor, progressive tax rates, support for small businesses and worker protection rights. Already facing increasing economic hardship, they were pushed deeper into crisis as living standards collapsed, unemployment rose, and inflation averaged 150 per cent.

Although Williamson later opposed Washington Consensus policies (his paper does not call for a minimalist state or a reduction in tax burdens), his formulation came to be regarded as a 'manifesto for capitalist economic development', steering struggling economies emerging from a long spell of military dictatorship towards a strongly market-based approach based on the three pillars of fiscal austerity, privatization and market liberalization.[1] Such policies normally include the withdrawal of the state from economic activities; the closure or downgrading of state marketing boards; the privatization of state industries; the reduction or removal of subsidies; the elimination of import controls; the reduction of import tariffs; a re-orientation towards exports; tax reform; cuts in government spending; and investment liberalization and deregulation.

As this new economic paradigm was applied to tradable goods, services and intellectual property, the ability of national governments to protect local industry and food security, to insist on labor laws and environmental standards, to safeguard the traditional use of agricultural and medicinal plants, and to provide public services, was dramatically undermined.

Elements of these reform packages were adopted (by wealthy countries such as New Zealand/Aotearoa) or, under the new phenomenon of structural adjustment policies or SAPs, imposed on poorer, cash-strapped countries, often as conditions attached to loans from the international financial institutions, to debt cancellation or to aid packages. In Mali, for example, the World Bank made its aid conditional on the privatization of the public sector (including electricity and the cotton industry). In Zambia, following over a decade of enforced privatization and economic liberalization, employment rates dropped, manufacturing industry collapsed and food insecurity increased. As the European Network on Debt and Development (EURODAD) submitted in 2005, the IMF 'imposes excessively rigid macroeconomic conditions on countries, not only restricting a country's ability to determine its own macroeconomic framework, but often hampering growth and poverty reduction'.[2] Or, as economist Jeffrey Sachs famously said, it's 'belt-tightening for people who cannot afford belts'.

The relaxation of labor and environmental legislation may well suit large transnational corporations and a small, wealthy élite in the affected countries, but poor nations end up competing with each other to provide the cheapest workforces and the most amenable labor and environmental conditions – leaving large numbers of their people locked into a precarious hand-to-mouth existence. While rich countries and the newly industrialized countries of Asia had been able to protect their own industries at crucial stages of their development, poorer countries now found themselves denied the right to nurture their vulnerable agriculture, industrial and service sectors before they were exposed to international competiton. Increasingly reliant on a largely unregulated export sector, they were forced to compete in a global market that deemed any attempt to protect their own fledgling industries to be 'barriers to free trade'.

Free trade zones

The dominant neoliberal economic recipe was applied in countries across the world, regardless of local conditions – yet in many cases it was an abject failure. Repeated studies showed whole nations to be no better off and some decidedly worse off following their subjection to the IMF/World Bank-prescribed medicine. After an initial period of growth, Argentina, the so-called 'poster boy of the Latin American economic revolution', came crashing down in 2002. Despite a raft of policy reforms, many sub-Saharan African economies simply failed to take off, further increasing their reliance on aid and debt-rescheduling programs. Côte d'Ivoire received no less than 26 structural adjustment loans from the World Bank and the IMF during the 1980s and 1990s. The result? Per-capita income went into freefall in what New York University economist William Easterly describes as 'one of the worst and longest depressions in economic history'. The overambitious reforms of shock therapy and structural adjustment, he wrote, 'were the flight of Icarus for the World Bank and the IMF. Aiming for the sun, they instead descended into a sea of failure.'[3]

Williamson himself summarized the overall results on growth, employment and poverty reduction in many countries as 'disappointing, to say the least'. Meanwhile, the countries that have achieved spectacular economic growth – especially China and India – have done so in large part because they have retained high levels of protectionism and extensive industrial policy planning, and have resisted wholesale privatization. Nevertheless, the integration of global markets remains a core policy goal, even if it is enacted no longer on a broader, multilateral stage but rather on the smaller platform of regional and bilateral agreements.

As the latest WTO Doha Round remains stagnant, multilateral agreements have been sidelined by a plethora of regional trade agreements. As of 15 January 2012, some 350 regional trade agreements are in operation throughout the world, including the European Union, the European Free Trade Association (EFTA), the North American Free Trade Agreement (NAFTA), the Association of Southeast Asian Nations (ASEAN), the Southern Common Market (MERCOSUR) and the Common Market for Eastern and Southern Africa (COMESA).

These agreements are basically free trade zones made up of various combinations of countries in often-unequal relationships – invariably stronger partners have a greater role setting the rules. NAFTA, for example, signed in 1994 by the governments of the US, Canada and Mexico, was supposed to boost employment and strengthen all signatory countries. But the devil is in the detail. Local laws can be overturned since transnational corporations have the authority to challenge legislation seen as a barrier to their profitability. In one such instance, the US state of California attempted to ban MTBE, a toxic gasoline additive. The Canadian manufacturer sued the state for nearly $1 billion. In Mexico, while exports of farm products to the US rose from $3.2 billion in 1993 to $6.2 billion in 2001, imports of US farm goods to Mexico, including cheap corn, skyrocketed. By one estimate, between 1999 and 2001 US corn was sold in Mexico at prices 30 per cent or more below the cost of production. According to a 2004 report by the Carnegie Endowment for International Peace, while growth in trade led to an increase of 500,000 jobs in manufacturing from 1994 to 2002, in the agricultural sector 1.3 million jobs were lost over the same period.[4]

Trade liberalization has contributed to unprecedented levels of women entering the formal labor force in what are termed 'Least Developed Countries' or LDCs – usually in low-paid jobs. Despite the increasing feminization of the workforce, there is little evidence of new women-friendly social policies or of the extension of existing work benefits to this new category of industrial workers. The gender wage gap remains large in most countries – between 30 and 40 per cent in Asia – even where there has been rapid growth in exports reliant on female labor.

The 'folks' on the farm

Underpinning all these policies enacted under the banner of free trade is farmers' increasing reliance on producing cash crops for export. This is invariably promoted by its advocates as an 'opportunity' to give small farmers the 'freedom' to participate in the global economy, and a route to food security, more jobs and unprecedented amounts of foreign exchange. Yes? No. The evidence instead points to growing farmer debt, the increased use of pesticides and more farmers abandoning their land. 'What has happened is quite contradictory to (the) expectations,' says agricultural professor Deva Eswara Reddy: 'Globalization has resulted in the decline of household subsistence production. People look for greener pastures in other countries as laborers. Rural demographics are changing. While men leave, women are forced to reduce farming.'[5]

Farmers and rural communities are also threatened by the implementation of the WTO Agreement on Trade Related Aspects of Intellectual Property Rights (TRIPS) which effectively privatizes the practice and exchange of traditional knowledge. Farmers who have been growing crops from seeds for generations – up to 1.4 billion people in developing countries are said to depend on farm-saved seeds as the primary source for their next crops – now face legal challenges from big companies. Meanwhile native seeds are being replaced by new hybrids which cannot be saved and need to be purchased afresh every season. Even these hybrids are vulnerable to pest attacks – spending on pesticides in some countries has increased by 2,000 per cent.

A five-year review of Zimbabwe, Uganda, Bangladesh, Mexico and the Philippines – all countries that had followed structural adjustment policies – found that reducing direct state involvement in agricultural inputs, removing subsidies and liberal-izing trade in agricultural commodities, had only exacerbated the economic struggle of farmers. In Zimbabwe, in 1997-99, a shift to tradable horticultural products resulted in inadequate maize production. At the same time the costs of seeds and fertilizer soared – fertilizer prices shooting up over 300 per cent after the removal of state subsidies. Farmers' ability to 'compete' was further hindered by government cuts in spending on roads and transport systems, lack of credit and, with the demise of state marketing boards, lack of information.[6]

In Bangladesh, crop sector profitability declined throughout the 1990s at the same time as prices of fertilizer, seeds and irrigation equipment leapt up in price. In Mexico, the findings revealed significant deterioration in the livelihoods of small producers as state services were dismantled, subsidies for rural production were withdrawn, affordable credit became increasingly difficult to obtain and production costs soared.

Throughout Africa investment in agricultural research fell, while the dismantling of state-controlled marketing boards forced farmers to engage directly with a global commodities market of which they have

Our bitter treat

Our sweetest treat is tainted by the widespread use of slave labor. Current estimates tell us that more than 1.8 million children in West Africa, 400,000 of whom are under 12 years old, are involved in growing cocoa. While the number of children employed in cocoa farming appears to be decreasing, researchers at Tulane University in the US have calculated that, during a 12-month period in 2007 and 2008, 819,921 children were working on cocoa farms in Côte d'Ivoire (source of about 35 per cent of the world's cocoa production) and 997,357 were doing so in Ghana. Attempts to stop the practice have been ineffective. In 2001, a voluntary code of practice, called the Harkin-Engel Protocol, was adopted by large chocolate brands with the stated aim of removing slave labor from the supply chain by 2005.

The deadline came and went with no change. At the same time, according the USDA Economic Research Service, cocoa imports to the US soared from 999,600 tons in 2001 to 1,222,300 tons in 2011. A subsequent goal, to certify half of all cocoa farms as free from child labor by 2008, similarly missed its target.

While the US has invested in rescue and remediation to help victims of abuse, there remains a clear need for the large companies that dominate the cocoa industry, such as Nestlé and Cadbury, to ensure their cocoa sources are slave-free. But who is going to enforce such a requirement? In 2008, in a public response to an International Labor Rights Forum action, Cargill, a major cocoa trader, admitted that it did not have sufficient 'market incentive' to eliminate slavery from its supply chain.[8] The Tulane University report, published by the Payson Center for International Development, states that one of the most effective ways to eliminate forced and child labor in cocoa production is through the use of independent, third-party certification systems such as Fairtrade (as opposed to companies' own first-party efforts). ∎

little experience and with which they are too small, too poor and too scattered to adequately engage.

Take Malawi. Under pressure from the World Bank, this predominantly rural country cut back on government fertilizer subsidies at the same time as farmers were encouraged to shift to growing cash crops for export, meaning that food imports became reliant on foreign-exchange earnings. After a disastrous corn harvest in 2005, almost 5 million of Malawi's 13 million people needed emergency food aid. The country's newly elected president Bingu wa Mutharika then decided to reverse the policy. The introduction of seed and fertilizer subsidies, abetted by good rains, helped farmers to produce record-breaking corn harvests in 2006 and 2007. The prevalence of acute child malnutrition has fallen sharply and Malawi recently turned away emergency food aid.[7]

As the five-year study concluded: 'The agricultural sector reforms have not, on the whole, improved the well-being of those living in the rural sector... Even where produce prices rose, the cost of production rose higher.' This is a lofty way of describing the disastrous reality of extreme poverty and undernutrition that continue to mark the lives of so many of the world's rural poor.

'You liberalize, we subsidize'

While food security is undermined by increasing pressure to replace sustainable agriculture with cash crops for export, domestic sales are undercut by the ability of wealthier countries to dump agricultural exports on already vulnerable markets. As former World Bank chief economist Joseph Stiglitz writes: 'While blanket protectionism has often not worked for countries that have tried it, neither has rapid trade liberalization. Forcing a developing country to open itself up to imported products that would compete with those produced by certain of its industries, industries that were dangerously vulnerable to competition from much stronger counterpart industries in other countries, can have disastrous consequences.'[1]

Over the past three decades, Majority World countries have been forced to reduce subsidies, prohibit quantitative restrictions of imports and progressively reduce their tariffs. At the same time, wealthier countries continue to maintain high – not as high as they were but still high – support for their agriculture sectors, as permitted under the framework of the WTO's Agreement on Agriculture (AoA). Established in 1995, the AoA allows developed countries to increase their domestic subsidies (instead of reducing them), continue with their export subsidies and provide special protection to farmers in times of increased imports and diminished domestic prices. As a result, farmers in some of the world's poorest countries, hoping to benefit from expanded exports to richer markets (agriculture is, after all, one area where these countries are believed to have a comparative advantage) are facing severe and often damaging competition from imports often artificially cheapened through subsidies. As of 2002, for example, the Indian government claimed to have lost revenues of $1.3 billion, the Argentinean government $1 billion and the Brazilian government $620 million as a result of US cotton subsidies. That same year Mali received $37 million in aid but lost $43 million from lower

Agricultural subsidies – producer support as % of gross farm receipts

	2004	2005	2006	2007	2008	2009	2010	2011
Australia	3	4	5	5	4	3	3	3
Canada	20	21	21	16	13	17	17	14
Chile	5	5	4	4	3	6	3	4
Iceland	66	67	64	56	52	51	47	44
Japan	56	54	52	47	48	49	53	52
Korea	61	60	59	57	46	51	45	53
Mexico	12	13	13	13	12	14	12	12
New Zealand	1	1	1	1	1	0	1	1
Norway	66	66	64	55	59	61	61	58
Switzerland	69	66	65	49	56	60	54	54
Turkey	32	33	33	26	26	28	26	20
United States	16	15	11	10	9	11	8	8
EU27	33	30	29	23	22	23	20	18
OECD- Total	30	29	26	22	21	23	20	19

Source: OECD, 2012

export revenues caused by other producer countries' cotton subsidies. The Food and Agriculture Organization has acknowledged that, if all trade-distorting policies were eliminated, the world price for cotton would have risen between 3.1 and 4.8 per cent. The World Bank estimates that cotton prices could increase by as much as 13 per cent if all subsidies were eliminated.

Such numbers have an awful predictability. Government support for agriculture in the mostly rich countries of the OECD amounted to $252 billion in 2011, or 19 per cent of total farm receipts. In other words, roughly one in five dollars received by OECD farmers was a direct or indirect subsidy from their governments. Every cow in Europe receives more money in EU subsidies per day (an average of $2.20) than 20 per cent of the world's people earn as a daily

City drift

Farmers in the Majority World who find themselves unable to compete in a global market distorted by speculation, as well as by subsidized produce from rich countries, are left with few options. They may well be unable to diversify into other crops thanks to rural underdevelopment, inadequate transport systems, lack of investment in research, lack of credit, degraded soils and limited access to markets. The only recourse for farmers is to reduce costs, cut wages or plant more crops, which means more work, more expenditure (and therefore more debt), less land for subsistence farming and a greater toll on the environment. For many, particularly men, the only real alternative is to try to find employment in the cities.

Over the last 50 years, Mumbai's population has grown from 1.5 million to 12.5 million and São Paulo's from 1.3 million to 10 million. In Latin America and the Caribbean, 75.8 per cent of the population is classified as urban. By 2020, Africa's urban population is expected to exceed its rural population. And by 2025 the urban population in the Majority World is expected to be twice what it was at the turn of the century. Cities are centers of innovation, growth and finance. When coupled with a productive agricultural sector and a tier of secondary cities to facilitate rural-urban interactions, writes Nordic Africa Institute professor Fantu Cheru, they can be productive and manageable. But when

income. Rich countries currently spend about 10 times more subsidizing their own farmers than they give to the poorest countries in aid. Some of this aid actually consists of food surpluses that are shipped across the world and dropped into poor countries, where they price local farmers out of the market.

This toxic combination of ongoing protection in rich countries and further liberalization in poor countries has resulted in a surge of imports to many countries of the Global South. In a word, this is 'dumping' – it means that, although their products' export price is below the cost of production, farmers and companies in developed countries are still able to make a profit because their revenues are pumped up by subsidies. Farmers in developing countries, meanwhile, lose export opportunities not just because their access to markets in the rich world is blocked but

urban drift arises from the direct immigration of a desperately poor agricultural sector, as seen in sub-Saharan Africa, low-income Asia and Central America, the result is a long tail of unemployment, a burgeoning informal sector, deteriorating infrastructure, overcrowding, environmental degradation, the fragmentation of families, the dissolution of cultural identity and expanding slum populations. Poverty is becoming an urban phenomenon.[10]

This kind of urban migration also results in a fall in agricultural production, an increasing workload for women and an ongoing lack of investment in rural regions. All of which gives further impetus to calls to strengthen the position and financial security of smallholder farmers. In a list of recommendations to assist small farmers, Robert T Watson, director of the International Assessment of Agricultural Science and Technology for Development, suggests strengthening development-oriented local governance and institutions such as co-operatives and farmer organizations; supporting small-scale producers and entrepreneurs to capture and add value to existing farming and non-farming opportunities; and creating opportunities for innovation and entrepreneurship that explicitly target poor farmers and rural laborers. All of this will require substantial investment – not least in natural resources such as land and water.[11] ■

because markets at home and elsewhere are flooded by 'dumped' goods. Take Jamaica, an island country well suited to dairy production In the 1960s, it had 4,000 small dairy farmers and 80,000 hectares of improved pasture. Around 40 years later, there were less than 200 dairy farmers. Although most of these are small farmers, 50 per cent of the milk production comes from two corporate farms. According to the Jamaica Dairy Farmers Federation, cheap imports of subsidized milk powder from the EU, following the lifting of trade restrictions in 1992, saw the market for local fresh milk shrink from 38 million liters in 1993 to 18 million liters in 2002. In some cases, the unsold milk was thrown away. Farmers either cut back production or went out of business.

Unfair tariffs, export dumping and agricultural subsidies to farmers in industrialized countries have all been blamed for deepening poverty in developing countries.

Martin Khor from Third World Network concludes that WTO rules need to be changed to eliminate or phase out export subsidies and domestic support in developed countries; trade-related conditions imposed by international financial institutions need to be changed to protect farmers; regional and bilateral free trade agreements should allow developing countries to maintain tariffs that enable their farmers to retain and improve their sources of livelihood; and farmers should be guaranteed a fair price for their export commodities.[9]

As mandated by the Uruguay Round agreements, fresh negotiations on agriculture began in 2000 at the WTO but agreement on the extent of subsidy reductions has not been forthcoming. A 2005 commitment to eliminate agricultural export subsidies by 2013 sounds promising but negotiations on domestic support (which is much larger than export subsidies) have not been resolved.

Coffee fix

The failure of conventional trade to meet the needs of the world's farmers and producers is vividly highlighted by a commodity for which the world seems to have an insatiable thirst: coffee. The ingredients of the coffee trade make for a toxic recipe – erratic prices driven in large part by the volatile New York and Intercontinental exchanges, increasing supply from some of the world's poorest countries, and small farmers increasingly reliant on the take-it-or-leave-it price offered by street traders.

Most of the world's coffee is grown on small farms of less than 10 hectares, usually family plots of 1-5 hectares, scattered across the globe's coffee-growing belt and providing an income to some 25 million farmers in 70 countries (dominated by Brazil, Vietnam and Colombia). But 'income' may be overstating reality. As one Mexican observer stated, 'the coffee-producing zones coincide exactly with a map of extreme poverty'.[12] This is not through lack of demand. Coffee consumption has almost doubled in the last 40 years (most spectacularly in Japan). An estimated 1.6 billion cups of coffee are downed worldwide every day. But it is the buyers, processors and retail companies that capture much of the value in the supply chain and even constrain opportunities for small-scale producers to obtain a larger share. Small farmers typically lack the capital to purchase equipment that would enable them to process their crops themselves.

What went wrong? After all, smallholder farmers used to reap reasonable benefits from their crop. Up to 1989, the coffee market was regulated by the International Coffee Agreement (ICA), which comprised producer and consumer countries and was managed by the International Coffee Organization (ICO). While there was evidence of cronyism and corruption under this system, export quotas were set for producing countries to determine supply levels and the price was kept steady within a manageable band of $1.20 to $1.40 per pound. After the ICA regulatory powers broke down in 1989, the market was glutted with coffee and world prices crashed, dropping from $1.27 per pound in 1980 to $0.89 in 1990, and $0.46 in 2001. A new ICA came into force in 2001 but it has no provisions for price regulation and, by June 2002, the real price of coffee was only 25 per cent of its 1960 level.

This produces the crazy reality that, while in 1992, producer countries earned $10 billion from a global coffee market worth around $30 billion, in 2002, they earned less than $6 billion from a market that had doubled in size. Their share of coffee revenue fell from 33 per cent to less than 10 per cent. Coffee earnings in Central American countries fell from $1,700 million in 1999-2000 to $938 million in 2000-1. Some 500 families a week were by then migrating out of Chiapas in southern Mexico in search of work in the cities. In Ethiopia, where coffee accounts for over 50 per cent of export revenue, coffee exports fell in one year from $257 million to $149 million.

As more countries were incentivized to turn to coffee, global over-supply exerted further pressure on prices. Vietnam, a relative newcomer to large-scale coffee production, grew its output from 1.5 million (60-kilogram) bags in 1992 to 25 million bags in 2012 to become the second largest exporter after Brazil. The fall in coffee price had a disastrous impact. According to the *Wall Street Journal*, 'the collapse of world coffee prices is contributing to societal meltdowns affecting an estimated 125 million people... from Central America to Africa'.[13]

Since then, reports from coffee-growing areas have a disturbing similarity. Families dependent on coffee for their livelihood can no longer afford to send their children to school. They cannot pay for basic medicines or even buy food. Hunger is a mounting problem.

Men are forced to travel elsewhere in search of more lucrative work, leaving women and children to take on extra duties on the farm.

With no job security, little negotiating power, and no land to grow subsistence crops, seasonal workers have also been hit hard. According to the World Bank in 2002, some 400,000 temporary and 200,000 permanent coffee workers in Central America had lost their jobs.

Since then a shortage of Arabica beans – the result of erratic weather patterns, decreasing yields from ageing trees, crop diseases and the growing popularity of the high-grade beans – has increased demand and sent conventional prices soaring. Between early 2009 and January 2011, the street price in Guatemala, for example, more than doubled from 640 quetzales ($84) for 100 pounds of dried parchment (the shell-like coating around the beans) to 1,500 quetzales ($191). Nicaragua and Mexico recorded similar price hikes. But the potential benefits of this sudden spike were

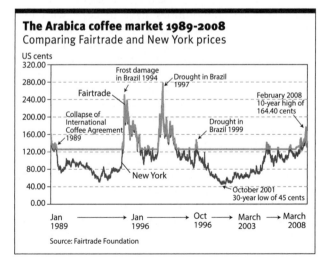

The Arabica coffee market 1989-2008
Comparing Fairtrade and New York prices

Source: Fairtrade Foundation

The problem with free trade

impeded by escalating food and labor costs, diminishing yields from near-exhausted trees and the enduring legacy of two decades of unsustainable wages. During the coffee crisis, coffee growers received just 1-3 per cent of the price of a cup of coffee sold in a café in Europe or North America and 2-6 per cent of the value of coffee sold in a supermarket. Following the recovery of coffee prices, farmers might now expect to receive between 7 per cent and 10 per cent of the retail price of coffee. A recent study of the value chain for Kenya specialty coffee to the US showed that some 87 per cent of the retail cost of roasted coffee is incurred at the roaster and retailer level whereas the price paid to the grower represents around 7 per cent of the retail value. A similar calculation for mainstream coffee to Germany concluded that 84 per cent of the roast and ground retail value accrued to the roasting and retail segments. About 6 per cent went to processing and export costs and intermediaries, leaving about 10 per cent of the roast and ground retail value for the grower. Even in the wake of increased street prices for coffee, coffee-farming communities have to cope with low nutritional intake and the break-up of rural families as older children are forced to seek work in the cities.

Choices are few. With limited access to local markets, and without credit facilities or adequate information, most farmers are forced to rely on prices offered by itinerant traders or 'coyotes'. That price is volatile and low. Climatic conditions and lack of finance and credit make conversion to other cash crops, such as cotton and sugar, difficult and many farmers cannot compete with more efficient and heavily subsidized US and European farmers anyway. In Peru, Colombia and Bolivia, farmers have switched to coca cultivation that will be used to produce cocaine. In East Africa, meanwhile, coffee growers have pulled up their coffee trees to plant *khat*, a local narcotic with a higher (and untaxed) street price than coffee.

At the time of writing, world coffee production is creeping back up, due in large part to an increase in Brazil's Arabica bean production. Prices will fall, and farmers will again be thrown to the wall.

Can the free market feed us?

Should we be worried by all these trends? Yes. World agriculture has to feed the 7 billion (and climbing) inhabitants of our planet and protect the livelihoods and food security of a total agricultural population of some 3 billion. World Bank figures show that 71 per cent of the populations of the world's poorest countries live in rural areas, where agriculture is the main source of income and employment.

According to agricultural engineer Marcel Mazoyer: 'Crisis and poverty were preordained the moment poorly equipped and unproductive small farming communities of these countries were exposed to competition from other far more productive agricultural systems, that had benefited from the agricultural or green revolutions and enjoyed other advantages of abundant land and low wages or subsidies, and the resulting fall in real agricultural prices. And there is no doubt that if the downward trend in real cereal prices (and therefore all agricultural commodity prices) continues, so will extreme poverty, undernutrition, hunger, massive rural outmigration and the escalation of urban slum dwellers.'[14]

In the market-driven commodities sector, agricultural prices are driven down to the lowest existing level, providing no economic buffer or financial security by which small farmers can invest in or develop their farms – or even encourage their children to continue working on the land.

The way to reduce the rural and urban poverty and the 'under-consumption and undernutrition that is slowing development of the world economy,' concludes Mazoyer, 'lies in a gradual, significant and prolonged rise in agricultural commodity prices in developing countries.' Such a step, he argues, would: increase the earnings of small farming communities and give them the means to invest and develop; curb agricultural migration and urban unemployment; raise the general level of wages; increase tax revenues and foreign-currency earnings in the poorest developing countries; and broadly revive world growth.

Continued free trade with its downward trend in real agricultural prices and its price fluctuations will condemn further hundreds of millions of small farmers and agricultural workers to stagnation, impoverishment, migration and hence to unemployment and low wages, especially in developing countries, but also to some extent in developed countries.

Complex as they are, and less easy to 'concretize' through a particular craft or imported crop, these issues were central to the emerging fair trade movement. Its member organizations and small farmers added their voices to campaigns demanding that developing countries be allowed to protect their domestic agricultural sectors on the grounds of food security and sustainable rural development and to regulate foreign investment in accordance with national social, environmental and labor standards. And in embarking on a form of trade that insisted on long-term transparent relationships based on fair remuneration, the fair trade movement, initially at least, set itself up as an alternative to a system built on the 'freedom' of the world's most powerful commercial operations to seek out the lowest prices at the most amenable terms of trade.

1 Joseph Stiglitz, *Globalization and its Discontents*, New York: Penguin 2002. **2** European Network on Debt and Development, 'EURODAD Submission to the World Bank/IMF', 8 June 2005. **3** William Easterly, *The White Man's Burden*, Penguin, New York, 2006. **4** nin.tl/11HlzUm **5** nin.tl/XHR8iA **6** Structural Adjustment Participatory Review Initiative, 2004. **7** Nancy Birdsall, Augusto de la Torre, Felipe Valencia Caicedo, *The Washington Consensus: Assessing a Damaged Brand*, Center for Global Development Working Paper 211,

May 2010. **8** nin.tl/10qFyep **9** Martin Khor, 'Globalisation, Liberalisation and Protectionism: The Global Framework Affecting Rural Producers in Developing Countries', twnside.org.sg **10** Fantu Cher, 'Globalization and uneven urbanization in Africa: the limits to effective urban governance in the provision of basic services', American University, 2005. **11** nin.tl/Yone5u **12** Josefina Aranda & Carmen Morales, *Poverty Alleviation through Participation in Fair Trade Coffee Networks*, Colorado State University, 2002. **13** online.wsj.com/article **14** Marcel Mazoyer, *Protecting small farmers and the rural poor in the context of globalization*, FAO 2001.

4 Is fair trade working?

Fair trade sales have been booming worldwide, even since the financial crisis of 2008. But is fair trade actually delivering for the small farming communities that are intended to benefit? There is a long enough track record now to judge whether the movement's achievements are matching its aspirations.

THE ORIGINAL GOAL of the alternative trade movement was to establish trading partnerships based on dialogue, transparency and respect; to use trade as a tool for sustainable development to help marginalized farmers and workers move to a position of security and economic self-sufficiency. This goal is evident in the WFTO's 10 principles of fair trade and the 'bottom line' of Fairtrade certification. Both insist on: a fair price that covers the cost of sustainable production; long-term trading relationships; access to credit; pre-finance where required; and additional support – including Fairtrade's social premium – to

From slum to school

What began as a recreation center to improve the prospects of 'parking boys' – street children employed to direct motorists to parking lots on the streets of Nairobi, Kenya – has evolved into one of Africa's most successful rehabilitation agencies. In 1973, the late Dutch missionary Arnold Grol launched a scheme to provide shelter and support for children working on the city's streets. Since then the Undugu Society (the name is drawn from the Kiswahili word *ndugu*, meaning solidarity or camaraderie) has worked to establish AIDS clinics, upgrade slum dwellings, set up schooling programs for primary school-aged children and provide vocational training and low-cost shelter for the homeless.

Today, Undugu Fair Trade, the trading arm of the Society, works with over 800 families or groups throughout the country to establish viable income enterprises based on the manufacture of intricately carved, distinctively East African soapstone carvings, animal hide drums, sets of wooden animals and elaborately decorated stone plates. From the

improve productivity and community resilience. In turn, producer groups are required to organize into democratically organized co-operatives or bodies; they must not use child labor; they meet or work towards standards of environmental protection; and avoid discrimination on the grounds of gender, ethnicity, caste or religion.

Gauging the success of fair trade in meeting these goals is not so straightforward. Fairtrade International data relates to certified products and producers, so leaving handcrafts largely untouched (even though craft-making provides vital income to women and disabled workers – often the poorest of the poor). WFTO-affiliated organizations and umbrella groups have conducted surveys but, without a standardized process, it is difficult to make annual comparisons. Many fair trade organizations compile first-hand accounts of the farmers and artisans with whom they work. Critics argue that these are anecdotal accounts – and shots are regularly fired across the bows of fair trade about the overuse of single-instance anecdotal evidence. But such accounts are at least indicative of

beginning, says marketing manager Fred Masinde, the goal was to sow the seeds necessary for economic and personal survival. 'Looking into the background of these children, always there was poverty on a family level. Often they were sleeping on the pavement – some of them would sneak back to give money to their mothers, who were involved in commercial sex. The priority was to give these children safety. But in working with children we were treating the symptoms – you do also need to look at the root cause, and that's where trade comes in. With traditional trading organizations, artisans were getting 50 cents for something that was being sold for 20 dollars – the artisan was really at the bottom of the supply chain. So, we thought, we can pay the artisan 5 dollars from a 10-dollar price tag and use the difference to support education and other social developments. This is about employment for people rather than depending on handouts. It gives them dignity. It's a business they take pride in – they can say that, with my own skills, I am going to feed myself and my children.[2] ∎

the desire to add a human face to the otherwise abstract supply chain. Others, such as Traidcraft in the UK and Trade Aid in New Zealand/Aotearoa, undertake their own social audits alongside their financial accounts to measure their performance against the goals of their charters.

Put them all together, throw in a few meta-surveys, and a picture of the impact of the last 10 years of fair trade does emerge.[1] There are blank spots: little appears to be known about the impact of fair trade on women, wage workers or temporary workers employed on smallholder farms. While Central and South America are well-documented, Asia, home to over a third of the world's poor, is the least-documented region.

But, whatever study you read, one thing is clear: fair trade is growing. The global market for Fairtrade-labeled products has grown at an average 30-40 per cent a year since 1998, dropping to a still-commendable rate of 15 per cent during the economically bleak years of 2008-09. In 2011, Fairtrade shoppers in 120 countries spent $6.3 billion on Fairtrade products. That year there were more than 1.2 million farmers and workers in 66 countries (most recently Guyana, Lebanon and Uzbekistan) making or growing Fairtrade products. Yes, in the context of the total global food and beverage industry, it is but a pinch, representing less than 1 per cent of total sales, but it is growing and the large companies that dominate this industry are taking note.

Is it reaching the most needy? Again, that is hard to gauge. In all the countries where fair trade goods are made or grown there remain large sectors of the population that are desperately poor, out of reach of statistical data, not organized into groups or co-operatives, eking out a hand-to-mouth existence. As one commentator said, fair trade tends to support those on the next rung up – those already working on farms or in artisan co-operatives, although anecdotal evidence suggests those who first established these groups and

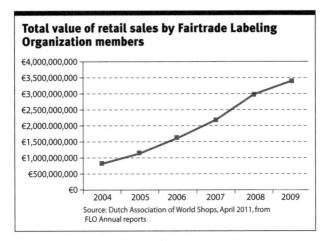

Total value of retail sales by Fairtrade Labeling Organization members

€4,000,000,000					
€3,500,000,000					
€3,000,000,000					
€2,500,000,000					
€2,000.000,000					
€1,500,000,000					
€1,000,000,000					
€500,000,000					
€0	2004	2005	2006	2007	2008	2009

Source: Dutch Association of World Shops, April 2011, from FLO Annual reports

co-operatives may have reached out to the truly jobless, homeless and income-less.

Cash is king

If there is any one impact on which all the studies agree, it is the evidence of higher and more predictable incomes among groups working within fair trade networks. Across the board, fair trade is shown to improve the livelihoods of farmers in sectors traditionally associated with low and highly volatile price returns.

This is most evident within the coffee sector. A 2003 study of coffee farmers in Mexico found that fair trade coffee averaged twice the street price available from conventional local buyers. A 2002-3 study of Tanzania's KNCU coffee co-operative found that fair trade participation yielded an extra $607,480 in one season – a 38-per-cent differential over conventional rates. In its survey of coffee farmers in Latin America, a Colorado State University report in 2003 states: 'All of the case studies demonstrate that Fair Trade improves the well-being of coffee farmer families and individuals... although poverty persists among coffee grower families, the standard of living among Fair Trade producer households has improved despite the dramatic decline in the global coffee market.'[3]

During the two coffee price crises (1989-94 and 1999-2005) fair trade's minimum or base prices paid to producer organizations for green (unroasted) coffee were well above the world price, as much as three times higher. Even in hard times, the higher price for Fairtrade coffee has meant the difference between survival and bankruptcy for many small farmers. And, when world prices climbed out of their six-year trough, there remained a small but persistent difference between the Fairtrade minimum price and that offered by local intermediaries or 'coyotes'. In 2011, Fairtrade-certified coffee farmers in Peru had a higher and more stable income than non-certified farmers. While these farms also carried organic certification, which carries its own price differential, the fact that they were able to increase production at a higher rate than the conventionally traded coffee farm is attributed to Fairtrade support.

While productivity depends on a range of local factors – topography, geography, soil characteristics, climatic conditions, different farming systems used – impact studies of Fairtrade certification on coffee and banana producers in Peru, Costa Rica and Ghana

Fairtrade premiums

Type of coffee	Fairtrade minimum price regular or conventional cents/lb	Fairtrade premium cents/lb	Organic premium cents/lb
Washed arabica	140	20	30
Natural arabica	135	20	30
Washed robusta	105	20	30
Natural robusta	101	20	30

Source: Institutional Trade Center, *The Coffee Exporter's Guide*, Geneva, 2011

show that, in most cases, involvement in Fairtrade also increased yields of key crops.

Higher prices have also been found to have spin-off, or 'halo', effects. In Mexico, the presence of Fairtrade has forced street traders to increase their prices. Similar effects were identified in Ghana, Tanzania, Bolivia, Peru and Nicaragua. Make no mistake, returns for basic food items fluctuate between low and lower. Even though Fairtrade International has adjusted its minimum prices for Arabica coffee, for example, twice in recent years, still the market value of the minimum price has declined – by an estimated 41 per cent – in real terms. Why? Minimum prices were never tied to inflation and income statistics are tempered by the fact that many Fairtrade-certified co-operatives cannot sell all their members' produce through fair trade channels (less than a quarter of the world's Fairtrade-certified produce is sold as Fairtrade) so forcing them to sell the remainder at regular prices.

Overall fair trade prices for agricultural goods are not transformational, but they are better – certainly in the cases of coffee, cocoa and cotton – than those earned in the non-fair trade sector (while cotton and cocoa fair trade returns are higher than their non-fair trade neighbors they are still less than they were five years ago).

In what will be a recurring theme throughout this chapter, such differentials were not so obvious in 'hired labor' (read plantation or estate) situations. A Fairtrade-certified Indian tea estate, for example, was found to pay its daily workers, who comprised around 90 per cent of the total workforce, the same monthly salary of $40 – just 77 per cent of the minimum daily wage in that country – as the comparison non-fair trade group. This was justified by the management of the company in question by the provision of additional benefits or 'in kind payment' – a roof to sleep under and food to eat. Worse is to come. A 2006 report by Hal Weitzman of the *Financial Times* claimed that

Is fair trade working?

'fair trade' workers on five Peruvian coffee farms were being paid below the minimum wage. After deductions for food and housing, casual coffee pickers employed during the harvest season were being paid well below the legal daily minimum wage for casual agricultural workers. Luuk Zonneveld, managing director of Fairtrade International, said the problem should be put in context. 'Poor farmers often struggle to pay their workers fairly,' he said. 'Why are casual laborers there at all? There are wider issues here. We need to ask why this goes on and what we can do to help.'[4]

The credit lifeline

Even in cases where the Fairtrade differential is small, many farmers included in the surveys highlighted the importance of credit, either as pre-finance, co-operative-run credit schemes or affordable bank loans, as one of the most important benefits of fair trade. For seasonal industries such as agriculture, and in times of disaster or extreme weather conditions, access to affordable credit is a vital means of investing in raw materials or new technologies and of tiding farming communities over during the lean months of the agricultural calendar. Even in craft-making communities, local microcredit schemes can provide the seeding finance for new agricultural ventures or investment in new equipment.

As Vi Cottrell, co-founder of Trade Aid in New Zealand/Aotearoa, explains: 'When fair trade is operating at its best, it offers people the option of doing something different. To me, the keys to that are the savings and the microcredit schemes. You visit a woman who began making hammocks in something like a chook-house and now she has a vegetable garden and she has goats – not a goat that some agency has given but a goat she has bought.'[5] And Fairtrade certification also gives producer organizations the credibility for external funding, since it is assumed that they are subject to external monitoring and that they have the required initiative to enter 'new market niches'. Still, such credit is not always available. Some farmer organizations have to draw on their members' cash, in the form of a delayed payment, to finance the business and manage price risk. This could be mutually advantageous but, as poor households rely on access to cash throughout the season and/or at critical times of the season, it has been found to be a divisive issue.

Any discussion of increased returns through fair trade has to be balanced against the costs of certification. While the WFTO mark is purely an organizational mark, with costs covered by the traders rather than the producers, Fairtrade labeling requires the payment of an initial certification fee, dependent on the size and type of the organization and the number of products it wishes to sell, and an annual flat-rate fee, as well as the costs of implementing the standard itself. The current flat-fee system means that farmers with larger asset bases are better placed to meet certification requirements. For many small farmers, even well-resourced and well-organized farmer co-operatives, certification is simply too costly.

A searing report in 2012 by journalists from the Forum for African Investigative Reporters (FAIR) claimed that the party making the most extra money out of cocoa sold is Fairtrade International itself, and that 'Fairtrade' farmers in Côte d'Ivoire, Cameroon, Ghana and Nigeria were not receiving more income for their harvests than 'ordinary' farmers. According to the writers, the Fairtrade model perpetuates traditional 'unfair' trading systems whereby the farmer remains at the bottom end. In response, Fairtrade International said that, while acknowledging there is room for improvement, co-operatives remain the best way to organize farmers and overcome these challenges, that fair trade is a 'process' and that the report relied on interviews with only 10 farmers anyway.

Is fair trade working?

Spending on the community

Even where fair trade offers only a small income differential from that offered through the conventional market, study after study points to the importance of the Fairtrade premium – a sum of money (a total of $84 million in 2011) fixed by the FLO Standards Unit and paid on top of the Fairtrade price. Fairtrade International offers some guidelines for the use of these funds – it recommends they be used for training courses, professional skills and community services – but the final decision lies with the farmer co-operative or, in the case of plantations and estates, with joint worker-employer bodies. Reports show Fairtrade premium funds being used for credit schemes, literacy projects, road-building, housing, health initiatives and training schemes.

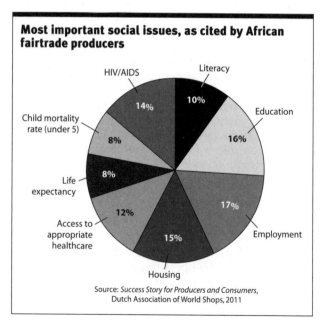

Most important social issues, as cited by African fairtrade producers

- HIV/AIDS 14%
- Literacy 10%
- Education 16%
- Employment 17%
- Housing 15%
- Access to appropriate healthcare 12%
- Life expectancy 8%
- Child mortality rate (under 5) 8%

Source: *Success Story for Producers and Consumers,* Dutch Association of World Shops, 2011

Most commonly, however, this funding is used for education: direct support for new schools, classrooms, school equipment and scholarships; and indirect support in terms of improved roads to provide better access and to attract teaching staff to often remote villages. In Costa Rica, the Coocafé coffee co-operative uses Fairtrade premiums to provide secondary-school scholarships and an educational fund for tertiary students. In the coffee-growing district of Badano in Ethiopia, coffee farmers in the village of Illili Darartu used Fairtrade premium funds from the umbrella Oromia Coffee Farmers Co-operative Union to build a primary school – in Ethiopia, once a community builds its own school, the government agrees to resource it with textbooks and teachers. The school now has a roll of 1,328 students. In Ghana, the Kuapa Kokoo cocoa co-operative has built seven schools and a pre-school center for farmers' families and local communities.

This focus on education has huge ramifications. In regions like West Africa where, as we have seen, children are still forced to work in the cocoa industry, the availability of – and commitment to – schooling shows a local determination to keep adults in the field and kids in the classroom. Even when incidents of child slavery on some Fairtrade-certified farms in Ghana, including a Kuapa Kokoo member co-operative, were brought to the public attention in a 2010 BBC documentary, these had been identified through the Fairtrade auditing process. The co-operative had been struck off the buying register while they dealt with the problem, the children enrolled in a school and the entire process used as an example of the effectiveness of Fairtrade auditing mechanisms in contrast to conventional supply chains.

This commitment to education demonstrates a resolve by farmer and artisan co-operatives that the next generation will have more choices than their parents had. It clearly negates the argument advanced by some that fair trade retards diversification and, as one critic had it, 'promotes continued reliance on products that are arguably poor prospects in the long run'.[6] This view is based on the argument that fair trade incentivizes producers to remain in sectors that offer little long-term opportunity.

I mention this critical perspective to Puneet Chawla, public relations person for Tara Projects in India. He is initially puzzled. Many of the artisans working with Tara Projects, he says, were already working in the handcraft sector before they joined the organization. Then, as part of the commercial sector, they had to work long hours for low and irregular returns and in a poor, often hazardous working environment. Since joining a co-operative that sells through Tara Projects, they now receive a more just return, fairer

Oromia

Botanical evidence suggests that, while coffee cultivation began in Yemen in the 14th century, it was in the fertile highlands of Ethiopia that the *Coffea* plant first grew wild. It remains a vital crop for Ethiopian farmers right up to the present day but for many years the majority of the country's coffee farmers struggled to cover the costs of production. Farms were isolated, the climate was often difficult and still the beans were priced on the unstable futures and commodity markets in London and New York with no regard to production costs. In 1999, Tadesse Meskela and Dessalegn Jena registered the Oromia Coffee Farmers Co-operative Union in Addis Ababa to provide a workable alternative to a global system that kept farmers desperately poor and denied the high-quality Arabica coffee bean the recognition it deserved. The plan was simple: to reduce the chain of intermediaries that characterizes the international coffee trade, to negotiate directly with importers and to sell Arabica beans through fair trade channels. Within 10 years, Oromia coffee sales had reached a record 6,400 tonnes (of which 60 per cent was Fairtrade organic and a further 20 per cent was Fairtrade). In sorting and exporting their own coffee, the 143 member co-operatives have been able to increase their income and use the added Fairtrade premium to build or expand schools, construct or resource health clinics, and put in more than 50 new water bores.

terms of trade, safer worker conditions, positions of responsibility in their groups, the opportunity to invest in savings schemes and access to training or literacy programs. Artisans with children, he says, are able to send them not just to primary school but also to secondary school and even to tertiary colleges – an option rarely available for craftspeople working in the commercial sector. If those artisans currently working with Tara have little choice in what they do, as a result of low or non-existent education when they were young or discrimination on the basis of gender, caste or religion, their children will have that choice. Yes, he says, some may elect to continue in craft work, and receive a living wage and the self-respect that results from engaging in productive and non-exploitative work. Others may choose to train for a different career. But they will have that choice.[7]

As Meskela told the UK's Equal Exchange in 2006: 'Because of fair trade we have schools in the village, because of fair trade we have health posts in the village, we have clean water supply stations in the village. Before, they used to walk 15-17 km to go to a nearby school. And there was no health center – people (walked) 15 km to bring sick people to the nearby health center. Because of fair trade we now have health centers in the village, we have schools, we have clean water supply. But this is only the start. There are only four co-operatives who benefit from the schools, only four co-operatives who benefit from the health centers. We have more than 100 co-operatives. Fair trade has to grow more.'[8]

To appreciate the importance of such advances they should be seen in the context of rural east and central Africa. Reports on coffee-growing communities in Ethiopia, Uganda and Tanzania tell similar stories of poverty and hardship: easily preventable or treatable health problems (malaria kills around one million African children each year because of lack of access to simple anti-malarial treatment), high rates of maternal mortality as a result of inadequate health, poor nutrition, lack of education, lack of access to clean water, poor roads and communication systems, few resources to deal with natural disasters, not to mention decreasing farm sizes as already small holdings are split amongst family members. ∎

Is fair trade working?

Fairtrade premium monies are frequently used to invest in business improvements: farming innovations to increase yield and quality, water storage, animal-proof fences, processing centers, new machinery and technological equipment, business training and improved quality control processes. In some cases the money is used to convert crops to higher-income generating and more ecologically sound organic production.

Information on the use of Fairtrade premium funds on plantations and estates is more scarce. The 2012 TransFair Germany/Max Havelaar Foundation study found that decisions on how to allocate the funds are more problematic where landowners live away from their farms, leaving paid workers from the local community to cultivate the land according to Fairtrade standards yet excluding them from decision-making processes. Not a shining example of democracy or transparency.

The Fairtrade Foundation also found evidence of farmers unable to access information on prices and margins in relation to downstream sales. Another study reported that only 2 of the 15 interviewed persons in communities supported by a cocoa-producing organization in Ghana knew exactly how Fairtrade works and that the community is supposed to benefit from premium money (although all inter-viewees knew about incentives such as cutlasses and fertilizers financed with premium money). In other cases, interviewees attributed Fairtrade benefits to international charity or merely to improved market access achieved by the co-operative.

Standing tall

While fair trade sales figures continue their upward arc, repeated studies show that non-income impacts of fair trade, such as engagement in decision-making and pricing, improved market and export knowledge, training and community improvement, are at least as important as the monetary return. Or maybe that long-term financial gain rests on a range of factors, not just initial price. According to historians Alex Nicholls and Charlotte Opal: 'The strengthening of farmer and farmworker organizations and their use of Fair Trade income to invest in community development projects can have even more impact than increasing individual incomes.'[9]

In forming democratic producer organizations, be it a farmers' co-operative or, on a plantation, an employer-worker joint body, farmers are given a voice in relation to debt servicing, co-operative management and expenses, community expenses and the use of the Fairtrade premium. The co-operative model also encourages the exchange of ideas, economies of scale, credit-worthiness, improved quality of produce, a stronger position from which to negotiate and a voice in wider public affairs. In more recent events related to the use and future of fair trade certification – more about this in Chapter 6 – farmer-run co-operatives are better able to represent the needs of members and establish their own commercial entities.

The importance of these aspects of fair trade is best found at times when the price paid to farmers is no different from that paid to conventional farmers. During the recent hike in coffee prices, fair trade coffee farmers in Mexico faced such a situation. As Eusebio Mejia Perez, a member of the ISMAM (Indigenas de la Sierra Madre de Motozintla) coffee co-operative in Mexico, explained: 'It would be easy for me to pick any old cherries, harvest them and sell my coffee to the coyotes, who would buy them from me on the spot. If I'm still with ISMAM, it's because I'm loyal to the group and I know I'm better off as a result of their projects; things like the cement I got to build my drying patio, the training I receive, and machetes I got for some of the work we do on the farm.'[10]

Is fair trade working?

Forging more direct links between producers and consumers further empowers farmers and artisans otherwise invisible at the far end of the supply chain. Visits by fair trade NGO representatives, buyers, inspectors, coffee roasters and retailers; the strengthening of rural networks; representation on regional, national and international fair trade bodies; respect for and acknowledgement of indigenous cultures and traditions; the increased social standing of women or other marginalized groups as a result of increased earning power: such improvements rarely figure in financial audits or annual reports but all are cited again and again as playing a role in improving farmer or artisan social standing and sense of dignity. According to a 2003 Colorado State University survey: 'Farmers' sense of their importance within their communities is often undermined by the increasing degradation of traditional lifestyles and the growth of rural poverty... But in case after case, farmers reported that the increased attention to their farming... promoted renewed pride in coffee farming'.[3]

Women benefiting

In fair trade collectives and co-operatives that insist on – or aim for – female representation at all levels of management, women assume a more active role in the economic decisions of their families and craft groups. According to the International Labour Organization, when women have direct control over income, they tend to spend it on their families and on what the UN Food and Agriculture Organization describes as the 'nutritional security' of more vulnerable family members.

Women dominate handcraft production, with approximately 80 per cent of the artisan co-operatives with which North American fair trade works being run by women. Some argue that, because craftmaking must be integrated into their daily duties, it becomes an added burden to already overworked women, entrenching existing patriarchal ideologies while men, unencumbered by childcare and other household duties, have the freedom to trade independently (and keep the income for themselves). While there is some weight to this argument, craft-making does give women an income over which they are more likely to have control and, in belonging to a collective or co-operative, they are assured a voice in the running of that entity, so 'expanding their economic choices, providing higher self-esteem and further developing their skills. Through small enterprises, women artisans are increasingly taking responsibility for project administration and are availing themselves of other programs such as microcredit and health programs that, in turn, increase their productivity and economic power.'[11]

Again, while women were found to be deeply involved in the decision-making processes of Fairtrade-certified coffee co-operatives, in the case of plantations this was not the case. The women did the physically hard work on the field and had sole responsibility for the housework and the children. On the banana plantation studied, female banana farmers worked 15 hours a day while male banana farmers worked 8 hours. Is this a cultural problem rather than one related specifically to fair trade? Perhaps. Prohibitive property and inheritance laws, lack of welfare, discriminatory religious codes, exploitative employment practices, systems of dowry, a workload defined by traditional gender roles and economic or social codes that regard women as a financial burden: all of these have contributed to keeping women in the world's worst statistics.

Further evidence of the impact of fair trade on women is found in the education of girls. In most parts of the Majority World, girls outnumber boys in lack of schooling statistics. In Africa, 41 per cent of

Is fair trade working?

Banning children's work

Child labor, banned by fair trade in all its guises, remains a persistent thorn in the side of the movement. Although child labor is prohibited under both WFTO and Fairtrade International principles and criteria, a study by TransFair Germany and the Max Havelaar Foundation found child labor on both Fairtrade-certified and non-certified farms and plantations, especially in the production of cocoa and cotton – and especially during harvest season, when most small farmers depend on their children's help in the fields. While interviewees recognized it as a problem, they explained that, at certain times of year, they simply needed their children's help on the farms. On the cotton plantation in India examined, teachers estimated that an average of around 28 per cent of the pupils in the surveyed village are absent from school during harvest season. In the comparison village where the cotton plantations were non-certified, this number rose to 60 per cent.

This is not acceptable by anyone's reckoning. As we have seen, fair trade speaks out against child labor, arguing that, if you pay an adult a fair wage, they will be able to send their children to school. But it is true that there is risk involved in ignoring the social, cultural and economic situation of potential trading partners. A problem with check-box criteria is that fair trade becomes a kind of blue-chip reward for standards already met. If fair trade is to maintain a truly pro-poor bias, then support by way of trade should be made available earlier in the process, at a time perhaps when a family or co-operative cannot afford to send their children to school, and when a long-term trading relationship can support such co-operatives to attain the goals they set for their members. ■

women have never attended school, compared to 24 per cent of men, while, in South Asia, 49 per cent of women have no education, compared to 36 per cent of men. Improving girls' education has been described as 'probably the single most important policy instrument to increase agricultural productivity and reduce poverty'. It leads to lower rates of child mortality, as well as better health, nutrition and educational outcomes for children (educated women are, for example, less likely to have their daughters subjected to genital mutilation) and plays a vital role in rejecting what the United Nations calls 'entitlements to violence'

– the belief in a man's right to physically punish his wife.[12] However carefully worded, no fair trade charter can 'fix' cultural codes that marginalize or oppress women – or, indeed, members of a particular religion or caste. But repeated impact studies show evidence of fair trade co-operatives using their funds to address the education needs and opportunities for girls and, through training, leadership roles and income, improve the social standing of women.

In Delhi, India, I meet Patassi, president of a 2,000-strong women's craft group working through fair trade organization Tara Projects. She is from Rajasthan, where life for women, she explains, is extremely difficult. But in coming together as a group, she says, women handcraft workers have been empowered both financially and socially. 'In the villages we do not even know how to speak to police. Today we can speak. Today we can talk about gender equity. When awareness comes it can change your life. Once you get women together as a group, in one organization, they begin to feel they should have human rights. So now we are more aware. Many women have not been able to go to school but now their children go to school.'[13]

Strengthening local culture

Fair trade has also been shown to help preserve cultural identity. In the villages of Vietnam, for example, the revival of interest in the art of hand-crafted lacquerware as practiced for hundreds of years by the majority Kinh or Viet people is regarded as a crucial endorsement of this unique yet marginalized culture. Tran Tuyet Lan, manager of fair trade organization Craft Link, says that the promotion of arts and artifacts made by ethnic minorities in Vietnam is having an undeniable impact on the artisans and their communities, not only in empowering women in their ability to earn a reliable income but also in elevating the status of those mainly elderly members of these communities who are able to pass on their knowledge to a newly committed generation. 'A lot of younger women are now wearing their traditional clothes again,' she says. 'They're looking at their traditions with new respect.'[11]

Real change is more likely to occur, however, when the producers are not simply at the far end of the supply chain, be it on a farm or on a plantation, but rather have a stake in the overall business. Some businesses and organizations have taken their fair trade principles to another level by being jointly owned by producers. As Tadesse Meskela told Equal Exchange in 2006: 'For fair trade to grow, to be fair, and for the price to be fair, producers want to have part of the profits of companies... To give back as a share to the growers so growers can grow a quality product.' As part of the

Indigenous initiative

In 1995, Aurora Maria Izquierdo, recently graduated from an agronomy course in the Colombian capital of Bogotá, sought the approval of her Arhuaco people, one of three indigenous groups living in the Sierra Nevada de Santa Marta mountain range of northwestern Colombia, to form a coffee-marketing association. After gaining the blessing of the indigenous leaders she set about organizing the coffee growers of her home region, Jeurwa, into a unified group. Within 10 years the Asociación de Productores Agroecológicos Indígenas y Campesinos de la Sierra Nevada de Santa Marta (ANEI) coffee co-operative was working on behalf of hundreds of coffee-growing families to procure a fair price for its members and to encourage more sustainable, environment-friendly methods of farming. Today many ANEI villages have their own community food gardens and water supply, and a new healthcare service has been initiated. Women are more involved in decision-making and the prevalence of violence and alcoholism is being addressed within member communities. One of Izquierdo's original goals, to promote and preserve the unique cultures of the indigenous Arhuaco, Wiwa and Kogui peoples, is also being realized. The use of traditional dress and language is more common, a number of *kankurwas* (traditional ceremonial buildings) have been built and the Busintana Research Center, aimed at reviving the use of native plants in traditional medicines, has been established. ■

structure of Cafédirect, formed in 1991 by the British organizations Oxfam, Traidcraft, Equal Exchange UK and Twin Trading, producer co-operatives are on the board and have a stake in the ownership of the company. Similarly, the Divine Chocolate Company was formed as a joint initiative by Ghanaian cocoa farmer co-operative Kuapa Kokoo, Twin Trading and The Body Shop in the UK (in 2006, the Body Shop donated its Divine shares to Kuapa). Fresh-fruit pioneers AgroFair and nut company Liberation are partly owned by their producer organizations.

On an international scale, in 2011, Fairtrade International granted producer organizations 12 seats in its 24-seat General Assembly, so giving producers a 50-per-cent ownership stake in the governance of the Fairtrade certification system. Similarly, membership of the WFTO board is made up of representatives from each region as elected by the member organizations, 70 per cent of which are producer groups.

The fastest knitters in the world

High up on the Peruvian Altiplano, Lima-based fair trade organization MINKA, Quechua for 'working together for the greater good of everyone', has worked for 35 years to help indigenous communities sell their range of unique crafts through local and international fair trade markets. The monies earned have been used to fund education, healthcare, roadbuilding and new income-generation projects. In recent years it has established a tourist trail to introduce visitors to the homes and studios of the local craft-making communities and to witness first hand the manufacture of toys, clothes and instruments made from clay and alpaca fiber. As founder Norma Velasquez explains: 'In Peru, those cultures and practices are disappearing more and more so we try to help people to be proud of their culture. It is having a very good result. For them [the artisans] it is very good to have someone coming over from the other side of the world. They say, "Why? Why are all these visitors coming to my home? I'm very poor, I don't have electricity or telephone!" Then they realize those people are really curious about their culture – that is very important for our producers.'[14] ∎

The price of a banana

The Windward Islands, a tiny arc of islands within the West Indies, are remote, hilly and – well, the name suggests the rest. Since colonial times, bananas have been grown here on small, family-run farms. It is a difficult climate, with extensive dry periods and hurricanes resulting in lower yields and a higher average cost than bananas grown on the flat, fertile plantations of Latin America. Nevertheless, the industry has played a vital role in the economies of St Lucia, St Vincent and Dominica, supporting the livelihoods of thousands of small-scale producers. But successive changes to the European Union banana regime from the beginning of the 1990s have steadily eroded the protection traditionally given to the Islands' producers. The replacement of the traditional quota system with a single tariff system flooded the European market with cheap bananas from Latin America and increasingly from West Africa. Windward Islands banana farmers simply could not compete with the resulting drop in prices. Between 1990 and 2009, the Windward Islands' share of the UK's banana imports fell from 40 per cent to 8.6 per cent. Compounded by global oversupply and irresponsibly low supermarket prices – the UK supermarket 'banana wars' in the mid-1990s cut banana prices temporarily to 43p (70 cents) a kilo, far below the cost of production and the prices have fluctuated since then – annual banana exports from the Windward Islands over the same period dropped from 274,000 tonnes to 82,000 tonnes.

Confronted with diminishing prices, increasing costs of agricultural inputs such as fertilizers, and extreme weather and disease in 2010-11, banana producers in the Windward Islands were driven out of the

The art of adding value

Reliance on any single crop or raw commodity is not in itself a recipe for growth. This is true on a national level – dependence on a narrow range of exports increases a country's vulnerability to economic shocks (in 2009, the export share of commodity-producing countries of the Global South stood at 30 per cent of GDP compared to 18 per cent in Northern economies) – and on a community level. In both cases the philosophy is the same, something to do with many eggs and one basket. To ride out the storms of price volatility and to increase self-sufficiency and food security, diversification and added-value processes are vital.

industry. In Dominica alone farmer numbers dropped from 11,000 in the 1980s to less than 700 a decade later.

Those that remained, however, were not going to go quietly. For years, Windward Island banana growers worked as contract farmers, selling their crops to private or state-owned banana companies which sold them on to the exporter, the Windward Islands Banana Development and Export Corporation (WIBDECO). In the face of strong resistance from the banana companies, growers, through the Windward Islands Farmers' Association (WINFA), finally won the right to bypass the banana companies and sell directly to WIBDECO. WINFA began working with fair trade organizations in the 1990s and in 2000 began shipping Fairtrade-certified bananas to the UK. By 2009, 90 per cent of Windward Islands bananas were sold to the Fairtrade market. In responding to Sainsbury's announcement to switch all its bananas to Fairtrade in 2006, Kenny D Anthony, Prime Minister of St Lucia, said that: 'In this era of competitive global trade, small-scale farmers like ours have little or no chance of survival without the kind of market intervention that is provided through Fairtrade.'

WINFA is now responsible for the whole banana supply chain from production through to export. With support from the Fairtrade Foundation in the UK, it is now investing in an agri-tourism venture and in a new processing plant producing juices, jams and jellies for local and export markets. According to WIBDECO's Colin Borton, 'Fairtrade has encouraged growers to discuss, consider and improve their farming practices... There is now an unmistakable pride by the farmers in their work, a concept seriously lacking in banana farmers before the introduction of Fairtrade.'[15] ∎

Does fair trade deliver on this front? Included in the WFTO principles of fair trade is the commitment by member organizations 'to increase the volume of the trade between them and the value and diversity of their product offer as a means of growing Fair Trade'. Under Fairtrade standards, producer organizations should 'promote the marketing of other crops... in order to decrease economic dependency on one single crop and to give the farmers additional sources of income.' There is evidence that this is happening. Fairtrade coffee co-operatives in southern Mexico and Central America are using coffee profits to diversify into alternative commercial crops and non-agricultural activities such as handcrafts. In Mexico, the ISMAM (Indigenas de la Sierra Madre de Motozintla) and UCIRI coffee co-operatives have diversified into cocoa, honey and organic preserves. CECOCAFEN in Nicaragua has invested in an eco-tourism project. Similarly in the Kilimanjaro region of Tanzania, the Kilimanjaro Native Cooperative Union has invested Fairtrade income into the Kahawa Shamba ('coffee farm' in Swahili) tourist project.

As was identified by the early critics of the economic theories of absolute and comparative advantage, the key to increased income is the ability to move further up the supply chain, from exporting raw materials to exporting processed items. In Uganda, on the lower flanks of Mount Elgon, close to the eastern city of Mbale, members of the Gumutindo coffee co-operative have constructed their own processing mill to cut production costs and to take greater control over their coffee quality. In the Dominican Republic, cocoa co-operative Confederacion Nacional de Cacaocultores Dominicanos, representing some 9,500 small-scale growers, has used Fairtrade returns to implement a fermentation program and to reach organic certification standards. It is now looking to export processed cocoa mass to keep more of the final product price of Fairtrade chocolate.

Many coffee farmers, particularly those in Latin America, augment Fairtrade certification with organic certification, so earning a further price differential and getting a second foot in the door of the increasing specialty coffee market. Throughout the fair trade coffee growing network co-operatives are investing in new processes, technologies and cupping facilities, and accessing advice from around the world, to improve their coffee in terms of taste, reliability and environmental sustainability.

---

1 Surveys used in this chapter include: *One Cup at a Time: Poverty Alleviation and Fair Trade Coffee in Latin America*, Fair Trade Research Group (2003); *The Last Ten Years: A Comprehensive Review of the Literature on the Impact* *of Fairtrade*, the National Resources Institute, (2009); *Making International Supply Chains Work for Smallholder Farmers*, the Fairtrade Foundation (2012); *What do we really know about the impact of fair trade? A synthesis*, the French Platform for Fair Trade (2010), *Pro-poor certification: Assessing the benefits of sustainability certification for small-scale farmers in Asia*, the International Institute for Environment and Development (2012); *Assessing the Impact of Fairtrade on Poverty Reduction through Rural Development*, TransFair Germany and the Max Havelaar Foundation (2012). **2** Interview with the author, 2006. **3** Douglas Murray, Laura T Raynolds, Peter Leigh Taylor, *One Cup at a Time: Poverty Alleviation and Fair Trade Coffee in Latin America*, Colorado State University Fair Trade Research Group, 2003. **4** nin.tl/10KK9WE **5** Interview with the author, 1 November 2012. **6** people.ds.cam.ac.uk **7** Interview with the author, 23 March 2011. **8** equalexchange.coop **9** Alex Nicholls and Charlotte Opal, *Fair Trade: Market-Driven Ethical Consumption*, Sage, London, 2005. **10** Trade Aid, *Pick of the Crop* newsletter, April 2006. **11** Caroline Ramsay Merriam, *Characteristics of World Trade in Crafts: Reasons for Crafts Program*, Co-operative Housing Foundation International, 2000. **12** *The World's Women 2010*, United Nations Statistical Division. **13** Interview with the author, 23 March 2011. **14** Interview with the author, 3 September 2009. **15** fairtrade.org.uk/producers/bananas/winfanterview

5 The world we live in

Fair trade's primary concern is with farming communities rather than the health of the planet but in practice it has proved to be a natural partner for the organic and environmental movements – and is helping to protect farming families from pollution and contamination as a result.

THE EARLY FAIR TRADE organizations paid scant attention to the environment. The focus was on workers – the artisans and farmers and the communities in which they lived and worked. But not for long. The environmental movement was born out of Rudolf Steiner's enduring theory of biodynamic agriculture and, from 1946, the work of the Soil Association in the UK, and was given a new shot of life first by Rachel Carson's seminal *Silent Spring* (1962) and then by the burgeoning interest in organics. This movement quickly gathered up the young alternative trade movement in its stormy march from fringe activism to mainstream politics. Backed by solidarity and anti-sweatshop movements, supported by a growing volunteer movement and increasing consumer activism, it provided fallow ground for fair trade.

As historians Alex Nicholls and Charlotte Opal note: 'The main ethical issue of the 1980s – "green" environmentalism – has now been broadened from a product focus into a more general concern over the entire production process, particularly highlighting the human/social element.'[1] The impacts of large-scale mining and logging operations and of plantation farming on water and air quality were not recognized by international trade structures. Indeed, in the bid to lure foreign investment, cash-strapped Majority World countries were competing with each other to lower the costs of production. With little to fall back on but agriculture, natural resources and cheap labor, attempts by such countries to boost foreign earnings in increasingly competitive and unregulated global markets invariably result in a catalogue of environmental degradation: exhausted soils, land erosion, air pollution, water contamination and loss of indigenous flora and fauna.

Around the world, the effects of reduced government control over agriculture and industry, and the pressure to increase export earnings, are evident in the increasing incidences of water shortages, deforestation, and the degradation of the land through salination and pollution. With the ongoing conversion of agricultural land for non-agricultural purposes (in Africa, Asia and Latin America public and private corporations are investing in millions of hectares of land to produce biofuels), small-scale producers and indigenous communities find their hold on land, and thus their future, increasingly precarious.

Across the globe, growing populations, climate change, the pursuit of biofuel crops and unsustainable agricultural practices are causing declining soil fertility, desertification and reduced water availability. The ironic result is that even the least fertile agricultural land now has value.

Such operations inevitably involve ongoing and uncontrolled deforestation, the unregulated discharge or seepage of pollutants into air, soil and waterways and large volumes of costly pesticides, herbicides and fertilizers. Sugar production, for example, is believed to be responsible for more environmental damage than any other crop. Vast habitats rich in plants and animals, including tropical rainforests, have been cleared to make way for sugar cane, and large areas of soil have been degraded through sugar production. Huge amounts of herbicides and pesticides are sprayed on to most of the world's sugar crops. In Australia, the run-off of toxic chemicals from sugar cane is blamed for extensive destruction of the Great Barrier Reef. In the US, phosphorus-rich run-off from sugar plantations is credited with destroying much of the Florida Everglades. The burning and processing of sugar crops also cause serious pollution of the ground, waterways and air, while intensive sugar cultivation can deplete precious water supplies.

The poor bear the brunt

While Western nations are able to maintain stringent codes controlling pollution, waste management and

---

The good bean

The small *Coffea* shrub is traditionally grown in the shade of a diverse range of native tree species, providing a vital resource for migratory birds, animals and even human life. Such an ecological structure provides favorable local temperature and humidity regimes, constant replenishment of the organic matter in the soil and a home for an array of beneficial insects that can act to control potential pests without the use of toxic chemicals. Over the last four decades, such holdings have been replaced by large, unshaded, intensively managed coffee plantations in order to increase the density of planting and produce higher coffee yields. And production has soared. In the last half of the 20th century, global coffee production increased by over 150 per cent. Of the 2.8 million hectares planted with coffee in Mexico, Colombia, Central America and the Caribbean during the early 1990s, 1.1 million hectares (about 40 per cent) have been converted to so-called sun coffee or 'technified'.

The most obvious environmental consequences of such expansion have been soil degradation and loss of habitat for birds, animals and, as smallholder farms are replaced by large plantations, people. In the coffee-producing lands of Latin America, deforestation has jeopardized atmospheric protection, topsoil and water quality, and has destroyed the habitats of many wildlife species (including bats, essential for seed dispersal and pollination of many tree species). As the density of coffee plantings on these plantations grows, and shade cover is removed, so their susceptibility to pests increases. New varieties of chemical-tolerant plants have been introduced that allow for the more widespread use of synthetic fertilizers, herbicides, insecticides and fungicides. The excessive use of fertilizers results in a decline in micronutrients, a drop in soil fertility, loss of biodiversity again and the pollution of farmlands

---

the use of chemicals in agriculture, much of the Majority World simply cannot afford to do so. Many poisons which are banned in industrialized countries are routinely used by farmers in the Global South – samplings of imported green coffee beans in the late 1970s and early 1980s revealed frequent detections of DDT, BHC (benzine hexachloride) and other pesticides banned in the US either because they might be carcinogenic or because they persisted too long in the environment. Yet it is in developing countries that the impact of such chemicals on the local human

and water supplies used for human and animal consumption.

The extra price and price stability associated with Fairtrade has enabled coffee farmers to resist the temptation to adopt higher-yielding, but less ecologically sound, monocrop practices. Unlike the vast unshaded tracts of commercial coffee farms, the smallholder coffee plantings that typify Fairtrade coffee are usually grown within a wide variety of food crops, fixing nitrogen into the soil, providing food for farming families and helping maintain soil fertility and local bird and animal life (in many areas where deforestation is a *fait accompli*, shade coffee farms provide a refuge for many forest-loving birds and other fauna). The inclusion of fruit trees in the shade canopy can also provide diversification of income and nutrition for producer families.

Fairtrade coffee farmers are also using the higher returns they receive to find alternatives to the highly polluting wet processing systems. Wet processing for red coffee berries improves coffee quality but the resulting waste water pollutes the environment and starves rivers of oxygen. In order to minimize waste water generated from processing, new water techniques are now being explored. In Nicaragua, where 95 per cent of coffee is considered 'shade-grown', coffee co-operative Promotora De Desarollo Co-operativo De Las Segovias, which works on behalf of 40 coffee co-operatives in the northern Segovia region, uses part of its revenue from Fairtrade sales and premiums to fund an organic production program. This has boosted its certified organic coffee production to nearly half of its total output. In recent years it has constructed a new wet-processing mill that recycles water and reduces pollution.

As more farmers convert to organic methods and certification, higher returns are invested in better education and health facilities, fewer families are forced to migrate to nearby cities in search of work and local cultural traditions are better preserved. ∎

population is most dramatic. Commercial agriculture in the Majority World is characterized by the close proximity of housing to fields and plantations, so leaving village homes and schools vulnerable to aerial spraying. Within rural communities the technologies used in the direct applications of pesticides – such as hand-held hoses – are often those with the greatest possibility of contamination. Little or inadequate protective clothing is worn – protective gear, consisting of boots, overalls, gloves, and goggles, is expensive and only of value when used and maintained in the right fashion. Information on the use and storage of such agro-chemicals is scarce or, because of low levels of literacy, unheeded. Chemicals are readily stored at home, pesticide containers are often reused for cooking and storage, and training and awareness programs are severely under-resourced.

Deforestation is similarly taking a disproportionate toll on poorer countries. Demand in Brazil for pig iron (a primary ingredient of steel and cast iron produced using massive quantities of charcoal), beef, leather and high-protein feed for livestock is accelerating the rate of illegal logging of the Amazonian rainforest. Some 20 per cent of the Amazon has been lost since 1970 – between 2007 and 2008 more than a million hectares of Brazilian rainforest were lost to illegal logging, soy plantations and cattle ranching. Such dramatic deforestation has reduced plant and animal diversity, compromised soil and water quality, forced native peoples from their land and put at risk customary knowledge related to the sustainable use of plants for medicine and food.

The Awá are one of only two nomadic hunter-gathering groups left in the Amazon. According to Survival International, they are now the world's most threatened people, assailed by loggers, hostile settler farmers and even by hired guns. In 1982, a World Bank-funded program allowed for the extraction of large iron-ore deposits in the Carajás mountains. The EEC funded the building of a railway linking the new mines to the coast (in return Europe received a third of the output, a minimum of 13.6m tons a year for 15 years). First the railway cut through Awá land and then new roads were added. According to Survival research director Fiona Watson, it was a 'recipe for disaster'. A third of the rainforest in the Awá territory in Maranhão state in northeast Brazil has since been destroyed and outsiders have exposed the Awá to diseases against which they have no natural immunity.[2]

Efforts to curb large-scale logging are being made, but too little too late. Brazil's National Institute for Space Research estimates that 6,238 square kilometers of rainforest was lost between 2010 and 2011, down dramatically from the 2004 peak of 27,700 square kilometers but still four times the size of São Paulo, Brazil's largest city. The same year, Brazil pledged to reduce deforestation by 80 per cent by 2020.

Fair planet

Fair trade actively discourages environmentally unsustainable farming and production practices. It discourages the use of agrochemicals and prohibits the use of genetically modified organisms. It promotes renewable energy, terracing, rotation and reforestation and encourages the conversion to organic agriculture. Under Fairtrade certification, both small producer organizations and plantations must comply with environmental management practices, including waste and water management, reduction in chemical usage, the conservation of biodiversity, the avoidance of certain banned pesticides and the safe use of permissible agrochemicals. The WFTO includes in its 10 principles the sustainable management of raw materials and the reduction in energy consumption and greenhouse gas emissions. Fair trade buyers and importers give priority to products made of raw materials from sustainably managed sources that have the least overall impact on the environment and they encourage the use of sea shipments rather than air freight.

Fair trade has still come under criticism for racking up food miles in the international transportation of global commodities but compared to conventional trade – which is the only relevant yardstick – its impact is far less environmentally damaging. As fair trade pioneer John Bowes explains, while 'there must be an issue about the long-term viability of commodity trading in luxury rather than necessary items', blame is more attributable to monocrop agribusiness with its trail of deforestation, pollution and lack of biodiversity. In supporting biodiverse farming systems, fair trade 'potentially offers an environmental lifeline'.[3]

On plantations the rules are not so clear. Rather than demanding new levels of environmental protection, as with labor standards, plantations tend to focus on the observance of national laws and regulations related to the environment. A Fairtrade-certified flower plantation in Kenya, included in the 2012 TransFair/Havelaar study, for example, had a robust system of training programs in relation to chemical usage and the importance of protective gear as required by the country's National Environment Management Authority (these guidelines, however, were more likely to be implemented on Fairtrade-certified estates than on non-certified estates).

Similarly, environmental programs in cocoa farms in Africa, particularly in Ghana, can have as much to do with the success of farmer field schools in West Africa – a South-South initiative that has resulted in increased yields, reduced use of chemical pesticides, diversified cropping systems and improved incomes – as with Fairtrade certification standards.

The small, often rural, co-operatives that produce the crafts sold through fair trade networks tend to rely on a dependable supply of locally sourced raw

The spices of Sri Lanka

Three decades ago spice farmers throughout Sri Lanka were burning their pungent crops. Prices paid on the commercial market were low, transportation was difficult and the costs of maintaining farms and investing in required irrigation systems were prohibitive. In the early 1980s, the small enterprise PODIE (the People's Organization for Development Import and Export), turned its attention from crafts to the country's struggling spice farms. To improve the living standards of spice farmers, PODIE sought new markets for their fragrant harvests of black pepper, cinnamon, ginger, cloves, chili powder and whole chilis through the world's fair trade markets. Today the organization works with 2,500 rural families throughout the southern and central regions of the country. By eliminating several links in the traditional trading chain, PODIE is able to pay farmers 25-40 per cent above market rates. It provides financial assistance for capital expenditure (such as irrigation systems, solar driers and drying floors), electricity supply and educational resources for village pre-schools. It also offers agricultural training for farmers, with a specific focus on environment-friendly and organic farming processes (it is currently running a cinnamon-replanting program). The PODIE name now extends far beyond the small villages of Sri Lanka. In recent years, the organic spices, particularly chili, have become popular with the Slowfood movement, a European initiative working to safeguard high-quality traditional foods and the livelihoods of small farmers around the world. ■

materials – wood, bark, shells, leaves, seeds and clay. Many of these co-operatives use the crafts and the promotion of these crafts to preserve traditional skills and techniques in the face of the increasing industrial production of crafts and the process of urbanization. In India, for example, the Sasha Association for Craft Producers, working on behalf of nearly 150 groups of craftspeople in West Bengal, Orissa, the Northeast and Karnataka, is working to revive the use of traditional medicines through the establishment of community-run health programs and a new herbarium where traditional herbs are collected and tested. Sasha also has four hectares of land on which villagers experiment and demonstrate techniques for organic agriculture and new methods of growing spices and vegetables.

In another initiative, Sasha 'adopts' about 20 farmers a year, providing them with seeds and information on agricultural processes. These farmers in turn spread their knowledge to other local farmers and villagers. Sasha has also helped form a farmers' committee in order to supply quality seeds on credit.

In Olongapo City in the Philippines, crafts made from discarded juice containers have become a source of income for local craftspeople and a way of cleaning up street debris. For over 30 years the PREDA Foundation has campaigned against the exploitation of children in the sex and other exploitative industries, offering rescue services, shelter and legal protection to the country's youngest victims of crime, as well as schooling, job training and employment. Since 2004, as one of its many income initiatives, it has recycled used juice containers, collected by local schoolchildren as part of an environment-awareness program. The containers are cleaned and dried at the PREDA Center where older girls are paid to sew them into strips. Local craftspeople then fashion the brightly colored material into a range of bags and hats.

Even the mere fact of addressing poverty works in favor of environmental protection. As Nobel Prize-winning economist Joseph Stiglitz says, poverty can lead to environmental degradation and 'environmental degradation can contribute to poverty. People in poor countries like Nepal with little in the way of heat and energy resources are reduced to deforestation, stripping the land of trees and brush to obtain fuel for heating and cooking, which leads to soil erosion, and thus to further impoverishment.'[4]

Going organic

A Fairtrade label does not guarantee that a product is organic. And organic and shade-grown labels give little reassurance about working conditions or farmer income. But the two have become highly compatible bedfellows, building on a conscience-driven form of consumerism and responding to the impact of non-organic agricultural techniques on the environment and farming communities.

Organic agriculture is a whole-system approach: it is based upon a set of processes aimed at a sustainable ecosystem, safe food, good nutrition, animal welfare and social justice. The International Federation of Organic Agriculture Movements, the worldwide umbrella organization, defines organic agriculture as 'a production system that sustains the health of soils, ecosystems and people'. Organic production is based on improving soil biodiversity and nutrient content. Better soils mean greater resilience to drought and other environmental stresses while greater levels of biodiversity in the soil and on the farm not only reduce vulnerability to pest and disease problems but also enhances the capacity to manage these problems when they arise. Organic coffee systems, for example, make use of shade crops, which in turn benefit bird life. Organic systems are also more likely to be associated with diversified crop systems as opposed to mono-cultural production (although this is not always the case for large-scale organic farming systems). Crop diversity improves resistance to disease and improves food security at the household level.

Supporting certified organic production has always been a good fit for fair trade. While organic production results in higher net revenues for small farmers in all the case studies reviewed in the previous chapter (with the added benefit of not having to incur the increasing costs of oil-based synthetic chemicals), when combined with Fairtrade certification, with its added premium for organic production, it adds further price stability as well as worker health and safety. Organic processes have also been found to improve yields through improved biodiversity, reduced pest and disease problems, better water quality and a more diversified farming system (although for conventional producers, conversion to organic is likely to entail an initial drop in yields).

Throughout Mexico, Fairtrade-certified coffee is almost synonymous with organic production. Coffee farmers associated with ISMAM, a farming co-operative representing 938 coffee growers in the southern part of Mexico's Chiapas region, close to the Guatemalan border, have been able to invest in organic production techniques with the result that their coffee is now 100-per-cent organic. Another coffee co-operative in Chiapas, Majomut, used part of its Fairtrade premium to hire a community organic farming promoter, helping farmers to convert their coffee and other crops to organic production. As a result, it sells 80 per cent of its coffee as certified organic. In 2001, it earned $1,700 from its organic Fairtrade-certified coffee harvest, three times the local street price of $550 (admittedly this was when conventional coffee prices were still in freefall). Technical advisors run courses on coffee tree management, soil fertility and conservation, pest management and harvesting techniques. According to Majomut's technical reports, the soil conservation measures of its organic coffee production program, supported in part by fair trade returns, has helped reduce soil loss from erosion by 3,800 tons per year.

Does certified organic production make sense as a development strategy? Benefits such as improved soils, protection of biodiversity and better water quality are critical for the future sustainability and resilience of agricultural production systems but these are often long-term strategies. In the short term, a shift to certified organic production for conventional farmers will mean learning new farming techniques while for *de facto* organic farmers this might mean intensifying production through the use of organic fertilizers, composting, green manures and biological pest control.

Organic certification can be costly and premiums are not guaranteed (unless combined with Fairtrade certification). Some argue that premiums for organic coffee do not cover the additional production costs or make up for lost yields and that the price paid by buyers does not reflect ongoing extra costs. Certainly, growing organically is a labor-intensive process. While the total cost of inputs may be lower than for conventional farming, labor costs are likely to be higher – an estimated three times higher than on conventional farms – due to 'initial adaptation work and... newer and more demanding methods of cultivation and harvesting'.[5] The transition period associated with conversion to organic agriculture can be anywhere between 3 and 5 years. For some, the expense is just too great. Consultations with over 3,000 farmers from 22 co-operatives suggested that 8 per cent of farmers in Nicaragua and up to 50 per cent in Costa Rica had ceased to farm organically.[5] Although premiums were in the region of 25 per cent, a premium of 40 per cent would be necessary for profitability. In Nicaragua in the 2007-8 season, gross incomes for non-organic farmers were actually higher than for organic farmers.

Shifting to organic production is also knowledge-intensive. For farmers who are used to conventional farming and have been reliant on external inputs, conversion to organic agriculture can take longer than for those used to traditional, low-input farming systems. Yet the fact that small farmers dominate organic production throughout the Latin American region (except in Argentina) suggests that small farmers may have a comparative advantage in organic production. Certainly there is a significant difference between shifting to certified organic production from a conventional intensive system – where high yields may have been maintained through use of agrochemicals – and working from low-input 'organic by default' farming systems, where practices may already have been environmentally sustainable, if not so economically productive. Many smallholder farmers do manage their land more or less 'organically'. Fertilizer and pesticide inputs, once subsidized by national governments, are expensive, and more traditional methods of farming passed down through generations are more likely to rely on alternative, non-chemical techniques for pest and disease control. Field research in the Rincon area of Mexico found that: 'all coffee plots... can accurately be described as "passive" organic because they use no agrochemicals'.[5]

While in countries with a long tradition of high chemical use, such as Kenya, Brazil and Costa Rica, the transition to organic production is more challenging, for *de facto* organic systems, the challenges may be less to do with changing farming practices and more to do

The cost of cotton

After China, India is the world's second largest cotton producer but cotton comes at a hefty environmental cost. Cotton is one of the world's heaviest users of pesticides and herbicides – in India, cotton production represents 5 per cent of total agricultural land use yet consumes 50 per cent of the pesticides used. Cotton farming in India is associated with widespread use of Bt (Bacillius Thuringienis) cotton, grown from Monsanto's genetically modified cotton seed, overuse of pesticides, indebtedness and related farmer suicides – an estimated 300,000 farmers took their own lives between 1995 and 2011. In 2009 alone (the most recent year for which official figures are available), 17,638 Indian farmers committed suicide. Two-thirds of farmer suicides occur in the five Indian states/territories that have come to be known as India's 'Suicide Belt': Maharashtra, Karnataka, Andhra Pradesh, Madhya Pradesh and Chattisgarh. The worst area is Maharashtra. In 2007, there were 4,238 farmer suicides in this state alone, accounting for a quarter of the total farmer suicides in India that year. These territories represent zones of highly diversified, commercialized agriculture where cash crops dominate – especially Bt cotton. Genetically engineered crops require extensive water or irrigation. They have much higher requirements for fertilizer and pesticide and, despite Monsanto's claims to the contrary, provide no guarantee of increased yields or profitability. Between 1996 and 2003,

with meeting the demands of different types of certification process. Of these there are many – different schemes exist in the US, Japan and Europe. Some can be arduous. Washington State University sociologist Daniel Jaffee cites the example of Mexico, where all food crops produced by a farmer, including fruits and vegetables for family use, have to be converted to organic in order to gain certification – a standard not demanded in the US or Europe. Similarly, rules prohibiting the use of animal inputs such as chicken manure as a fertilizer might make sense for European or US organic farming systems, but are not necessarily appropriate for the integrated, mixed small organic farms found in many poorer countries. Even when organic certification is attained, the threat of decertification is always hanging over farmers, 'and with

---

the price of cotton declined by 55 per cent, reaching its lowest level in 30 years in 2001-02, as a result of a massive increase in global cotton production and the 'dumping' of cheap cotton imports by subsidized nations (in 2002 US cotton subsidies totaled $3.9 billion, surpassing the total value of US cotton production of $3 billion). Also, unlike traditional seed, genetically engineered seeds are very expensive and, because they are sterile, have to be repurchased every planting season.

Rising costs of seeds, fertilizers, pesticides and other farm supplies, along with falling prices for farm commodities, regular droughts and poor access to irrigation, are forcing farmers to take out high-interest loans. When the rains do not come or the yields fall below expectation, they face the shame of bankruptcy.

The growing demand for organic cotton is hampered by insufficient supplies of non-GM cotton seed (70 per cent of conventional cotton in India is now being derived from GM seed) and organic fertilizers, lack of credit and limited development of organic farming techniques. Fairtrade-certified in 2005, Agrocel, co-owned by the Indian government and several small companies, has been working with small cotton farmers to build a market for fair trade cotton goods. Now working with 40,000 growers, Agrocel offers a range of support services to farmers, including farmer-to-farmer skills share programs, training and veterinary services for livestock. ∎

Delta crafts

With over 161 million people and a growing birth rate, Bangladesh is a populous country. Its population is largely rural and it relies heavily on agricultural commodities as one of its main productive sectors and earners of foreign currency. But it is vulnerable to severe environmental degradation. In this low-lying country, a one-meter rise in sea levels would flood more than 15 per cent of the land, affecting over 10 million people. An analysis of such a scenario by the Commonwealth Secretariat found that 10 per cent of the population would be displaced and land that currently provides two million tonnes of rice and 400,000 tonnes of vegetables a year, would be lost.

As with other Majority World countries, Bangladesh has been encouraged to invest in non-traditional cash crops for export. Today, shrimps are the third largest export earner after garments and jute, yet the vast areas of land converted into shrimp ponds exact a substantial cost on the environment. Peasant farmers have had their rice crops ruined and their fresh water supplies contaminated as salt water from neighboring shrimp ponds leaks into their soils. The development of shrimp ponds has also been responsible for the destruction of mangrove forests – either directly through the removal of such forests for shrimp or prawn aquaculture, or indirectly as farmers are forced to turn to the forests for their fuel or food. This is impacting heavily on the Sundarbans, a UNESCO World Heritage Site comprising a network of waterways and mangrove forests stretching across the delta lands of Bangladesh and India. This unique ecosystem, celebrated in a number of Bengali folk songs and dances, is essential for protecting the coastline from the extreme climatic events that plague this country – in recent years,

it the prospect of economic ruin. Each household must necessarily be concerned with the horticultural and production practices of other households, as the failure of any household to abide by certified-organic production norms endangers the organic certification (and product market prices) of all members.'[5]

Even Fairtrade requirements have been accused of being either too stringent or in some cases locally inappropriate. Fairtrade International, for example, requires growers to refrain from using herbicide on their farms to protect watersheds and aquatic life, but this has greatly increased labor inputs, as mechanical weed clearing has been adopted in place of the banned

heavy flooding has killed hundreds of people, and covered about 60 per cent of the country in water, while cyclones in 1970, 1991 and 2007 killed close to 700,000 people. According to the UN Environment Programme: 'Indiscriminate conversion of [Bangladesh's] mangrove forests into shrimp farms has resulted in the destruction of marine breeding grounds and the erosion of shorelines... A large number of local varieties of fish have disappeared and nutrient content of the soil has diminished, resulting in drastic reductions in land productivity.[6]

The sale of jute crafts through Bangladeshi fair trade organizations is providing an alternative and less harmful income source. Jute is completely biodegradable; no toxic gases or emissions are created in the production of jute items; and jute plants consume carbon dioxide, the main contributor to climate change. And, because it is a completely renewable and sustainable resource, the cultivation of jute poses no threat to Bangladesh's extremely fragile environment. CORR-The Jute Works (CJW) is a non-profit organization working with 214 rural co-operatives across the country to give women, particularly widows, divorcees and abandoned women, a sustainable income through the manufacture and sale of jute handcrafts. They use compost fertilizer made from cow-dung, water hyacinth and *doyancha* (a kind of water-sponge). Extracts from the neem tree, a fast-growing member of the mahogany family, are used as natural insecticides. To compensate for ongoing deforestation, CJW has now teamed up with the Bangladesh Jute Research Institute and Bangladesh Agriculture Development Corporation to establish a replanting program. As a result of this work, CJW distributes 20,000-40,000 fruit and timber saplings each year to its craft groups. ■

chemical herbicide paraquat. The mechanical approach has also exacerbated some weed and pest problems while also, particularly for older farmers, increasing wage costs.

External support may be critical for farmers who want to certify as organic – a clear and well-trodden path for fair trade organizations – but in the majority of cases, the conversion of traditional, small-scale farms to organic production, while incurring initial extra costs, does produce long-term improvements in yields and profitability as a result of improved farm management and practices as well as the price premiums they receive. If they find a buyer, that is.

Buyers from rich countries can be unwilling or unable to pay a high enough price to incentivize more farmers into organic production. In Ethiopia in 2010, for instance, farmers in one coffee-farmer union were certified organic but had to sell 70-90 per cent of their coffee at conventional prices because of limited demand among buyers for the higher-priced coffee.

When the rains don't come and the temperature rises

Smallholder farms across the Majority World share common characteristics: they are poor; vulnerable; often marginalized on the basis of geography, ethnicity and landlessness; and have a lower capacity to manage external events, be it sudden fluctuations in price or erratic weather and altered pollination or pest cycles. Yet it is here, in the growing belt of sub-Saharan Africa, the Middle East, South Asia and the small island states of the Pacific – the regions least able to afford costly embankments, new drainage systems, desalination plants and floatable homes – that climate change is having the most impact. A 2009 study by the Global Humanitarian Forum reports that nearly 98 per cent of the people seriously affected by climate change live in developing countries, even though OECD countries, with only one-fifth of the world's population, consume almost half the fossil fuels.[7]

In Bangladesh, for example, annual carbon emissions per person are 172 kg, compared with 9,000 kg in the UK and 21,000 kg in the US. Yet the poor have little voice in the debates on climate change. While Africa accounts for less than 3 per cent of global carbon-dioxide emissions, it faces some of the biggest risks from disrupted water supplies and extreme weather events. In Kenya, it is predicted that there will be a 30-per-cent reduction in the area suitable for the cultivation of maize, the country's staple diet. As Ugandan president Yoweri Museveni told the African Union summit in Ethiopia in 2008: 'We have a message

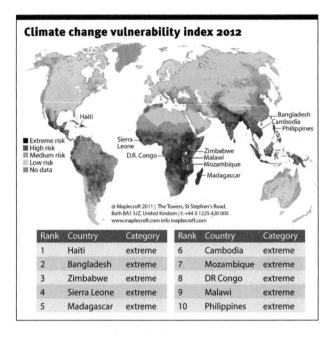

Climate change vulnerability index 2012

Rank	Country	Category	Rank	Country	Category
1	Haiti	extreme	6	Cambodia	extreme
2	Bangladesh	extreme	7	Mozambique	extreme
3	Zimbabwe	extreme	8	DR Congo	extreme
4	Sierra Leone	extreme	9	Malawi	extreme
5	Madagascar	extreme	10	Philippines	extreme

here to tell these countries, that you are causing aggression to us by causing global warming. Alaska will probably become good for agriculture, Siberia will probably become good for agriculture, but where does that leave Africa?'[8]

Coffee is particularly sensitive to changes in temperature. According to the Union of Concerned Scientists, climate change is threatening coffee crops in virtually every major coffee-producing region of the world. Higher temperatures, long droughts punctuated by intense rainfall, more resilient pests and diseases – all of which are associated with climate change – have reduced coffee supplies dramatically in recent years. In 2012, a study led by London's Royal Botanic Gardens at Kew warned that, as a result of climate change, Arabica coffee, the world's most consumed coffee species, could be extinct in the wild by 2080.[9] Already in Ethiopia, the world's third-largest producer of Arabica coffee, the mean annual temperature has risen by 1.3 degrees Celsius since 1960.

In Colombia, farmers are struggling with the impact of heavy rainfall, prolonged dry spells and lack of sunshine for the fourth straight year. According to CENICAFE, the national coffee research center, average temperatures in the country's coffee regions have risen nearly one degree in 30 years and, in some mountain areas, the increase has been double that, while rainfall has been 25 per cent above average. Increased temperatures cause the plants' buds to abort or their fruit to ripen too quickly for optimum quality. Heat also brings pests like coffee rust, a devastating fungus that could not survive the previously cool mountain weather. In Tanzania, drought led the Tanzania Coffee Board to cut production forecasts for the 2011-12 harvest period by 18 per cent. In Guatemala, Nicaragua and El Salvador, a new pattern of torrential rains is causing huge regional damage both to coffee crops and to coffee infrastructure.

Global prices for commodities such as coffee, tea and soy are woefully undervalued. They, and the mark-ups along the way through conventional trading systems, make it virtually impossible for growers and co-operatives to survive, let alone practice more expensive techniques that mitigate environmental damage. In contrast, rural communities are being supported in their bid to protect themselves, their communities and their crops by the growth of the fair trade movement, the relationship between fair trade and organics, the increasing contact between importers and producers, and the burgeoning awareness of shoppers and consumers in the Global North. Coffee farmers, often supported by Fairtrade International and individual fair trade organizations, are focusing on ways in which they can mitigate the effects of climate change while continuing to grow coffee. Smallholder producers and co-operatives are adopting new and improved technologies, skills and knowledge to manage increasingly erratic climatic conditions by way of water management, soil conservation and erosion control, crop management, pest and disease management, and renewable-energy technologies.

In Uganda, the Gumutindo coffee co-operative has had to contend with torrential rains, fatal landslides and an outbreak of leaf rust disease, thought to be caused by increasing temperatures and humidity that are in turn related to sudden climate change. New tree seedlings take years to grow and disease-resistant coffee strains take many years to develop and use. As Willington Wamayeye, the general manager of the Gumutindo co-operative told Justin Purser, food manager of the New Zealand/Aotearoa organization Trade Aid, in 2012: 'The rains do not arrive at known times and, even when they come, they are unpredictable and fall so heavily in a very short time, or they are so little that crop production cannot be sustained in the way we know.'[10] The co-operative has since launched a tree-planting initiative, distributing tens of thousands of seedlings to its members, and has provided training to farmers on tree conservation, protection of watersheds, keeping of wetlands and better general land management.

1 Alex Nicholls & Charlotte Opal, *Fair Trade: Market-Driven Ethical Consumption*, Sage, London, 2004. **2** *The Guardian*, 22 April 2012, nin.tl/10v82Qk. **3** John Bowes (ed), *The Fair Trade Revolution*, Pluto, New York, 2011. **4** Joseph Stiglitz, *Globalization and its Discontents*, Penguin, New York, 2002. **5** Emma Blackmore and James Keeley et al, *Pro-poor certification: Assessing the benefits of sustainability certification for small-scale farmers in Asia*, International Institute for Environment and Development, 2012. **6** UNEP, 'Environmental Impacts of Trade Liberalisation and Policies for the Sustainable Management of Natural Resources: A Case Study on Bangladesh's Shrimp Farming', 1999. **7** Global Humanitarian Forum, *The Anatomy of a Silent Crisis*, Geneva 2009. **8** developmenteducation.ie/media/documents **9** nationalgeographic.com/news **10** tradeaid.org.nz/reports

6 Just read the label

A label on each product guaranteeing its fair trade origin: it seems like a simple idea. But the fair trade movement has been split as transnational corporations have moved in for a piece of the action – and its future direction is still uncertain.

IT MADE SUCH SENSE. A certification label that would assure customers of a responsible and equitable standard of trade while providing a set of achievable and auditable criteria for producers. This was the thinking behind the development of the Max Havelaar Foundation, formed by the UCIRI coffee co-operative in Mexico and Dutch development-aid organization Solidaridad in 1986. The result, the world's first fair trade label, defined an alternative market channel that circumvented intermediaries and paved the way for more coffee to be exported under fair trade terms. Consumers knew the importers of the coffee had paid a fair price for the farmers' crops, they would be prepared to pay a little more and the labeled goods themselves could be sold beyond the existing 'alternative trade' shops.

The label spread, to Belgium (1991), Switzerland (1992), France, Luxembourg, and Denmark (1994). It expanded its product line to include cocoa (1992), honey (1994) and bananas (1996). Around the same time a group in Britain, including representatives from Oxfam and Traidcraft, established a national labeling intiative, the Fairtrade Foundation.

In the meantime TransFair, a similar but competing seal, had been launched in Germany and extended to Austria and Luxembourg. TransFair Germany brought in plantation tea, on the grounds that tea from small, farmer-run farms was unavailable. The Max Havelaar Foundation objected to plantation tea even being considered fair trade. The dispute was, if not resolved, then at least silenced in 1997 when the Fairtrade Labelling Organizations International (FLO) was formed to unite and co-ordinate the various labels and to rationalize the development of fair trade standards (TransFair's argument won the day and tea plantations were allowed into the system). The development of a new, widely recognized and understood label, with its distinctive yin-yang, green leaf/blue fish design, was also seen as a way to increase sales dramatically by distributing certified goods through mainstream retail outlets.

Formal certification arrived in the US a full decade after Europe. Originally housed at the Institute for Agriculture and Trade Policy (IATP), TransFair USA became independent in 1999. It joined FLO and quickly adopted a strategy of 'mainstreaming' to increase the volume of fair trade sales through conventional retail venues and under existing commercial brands.

In 2004 the World Fair Trade Organization launched its own Mark with a 'global journey' beginning in Mumbai and ending in Brussels in 2007. Unlike the Fairtrade label, the FTO mark is used to identify not individual products but 'mission-driven organizations whose core activity is fair trade'. In contrast to this more 'alternative' approach, FLO used its system of product standards and distinctive label to identify fair trade products within the conventional marketplace in order to increase sales and draw more producers into its ambit. As we have seen, sales of Fairtrade-certified goods soared, not just through alternative health food stores and fair trade shop networks but in supermarkets (led in Britain by The Co-operative and Sainsbury's), cafés, airlines and public institutions.

The Fairtrade 'brand'

Although it still represents just a tiny proportion of all global commodities, the Fairtrade symbol is today a recognizable 'brand' available across the globe. But it is not stopping there. True to its mainstreaming goals, the Fairtrade labeling phenomenon is in the ring with some of the largest players in the commodities sector. In 2000, Starbucks, the largest specialty-coffee roaster in the US (reeling from public charges of labor rights violations on its Central American coffee plantations), agreed to sell Fairtrade certified coffee at all of its US cafés. Initially accounting for less than 1 per cent of Starbucks' coffee purchases, by 2010 about 8 per cent of the coffee used in its global operations came from fair trade farms.

What does 'fair' mean in this context? Starbucks' overall fair trade procurement is minimal and critics note its long-term refusal to disclose information about the plantations where the bulk of its coffee is sourced. Also, while fully fledged fair trade organizations keep a weather eye on their own in-house practices, Starbucks is known to have massive pay and benefits disparities and a long history of opposing unionization among its staff (unlike WFTO principles, FLO standards do not impose conditions on the trading practices of organizations once they have purchased Fairtrade-certified products).

There was more to come. In 2005, the UK's Fairtrade Foundation announced that Nestlé – the world's largest coffee trader and food corporation – would receive the Fairtrade seal for its Partners Blend line of coffee. The Foundation acknowledged that certifying the corporation would antagonize many movement activists. After all, for more than two decades, Nestlé had been the target of consumer boycotts over its aggressive marketing of infant formula in Majority World countries – an international boycott that remains in place today. The Fairtrade element represented only a tiny percentage of the Nestlé product range – less than 1 per cent of the coffee it buys (some estimates put it as low as 0.02 per cent), and accounting for just one product out of a range of some 8,500. Nevertheless, the Fairtrade certification of Partners Blend coffee allowed the company to benefit from feel-good ethical associations with minimal effort, even though it had been the monopolistic behavior of such transnational corporations that had stoked the fair trade fire for three decades.

In 2010, Nestlé committed to converting all of its Kit Kat product line in the UK and Ireland to Fairtrade. Other high-street names came on board. Cadbury converted its Dairy Milk bar to 100-per-cent Fairtrade. The Hershey Company has announced it will source Fairtrade-certified cocoa for all its chocolate product lines by 2020. A number of mass-market coffee firms, including Procter & Gamble and, briefly, Sara Lee, followed suit, even though their fair trade sales volumes remained negligible. This heightened the profile of fair trade while frustrating long-time, exclusively fair trade coffee roasters who suddenly found themselves competing with the same brands that had traditionally scoffed fair trade principles – and which continued to source the bulk of their produce through mainstream channels.

U-landsimporten, then Denmark's largest ATO and the organization responsible for launching the Danish Max Havelaar fair trade label, saw its own coffee lines pushed off supermarket shelves by conventional retailers' Fairtrade-labeled coffees. In Canada, Planet Bean, a 100-per-cent fair trade coffee roaster, encountered difficulties persuading supermarkets to stock its coffee since many chains had opted to carry a single fair trade line distributed by the major Canadian roaster Van Houtte.

In 2006, TransFair Germany established co-operation contracts with German discount supermarket Lidl, previously accused of selling dumped goods and of violating their own workers' rights. According to TransFair spokesperson Claudia Brueck, 'the co-operation with Lidl is part of our general strategy to broaden the effect of fair trade in the German groceries markets. We are a product certification group but we do not monitor the behavior of corporations.' What? 'Ten years ago,' she added, 'the fair trade idea was a project of a few. Now, it has become a giant market.'[1]

In the US, Fairtrade-certified Honest Tea makes a range of tea-based beverages. But it is owned by Coca-Cola, which donated money to successfully defeat California's Proposition 37 initiative for mandatory labeling of genetically modified products in 2012. In launching a boycott against the brands owned by big-name donors that fought against the Proposition, the Organic Consumers Association wrote, 'It's time to raise a little hell.'[2]

Transnationals change the game

The involvement of transnational corporations was a marked departure from alternative trade's activist roots, when fair trade coffee, tea and cocoa was sourced solely from small, often marginalized producers who could not, and often would not, engage in a conventional trading system that pushed down prices and terms and offered no long-term security. The mainstreaming of fair trade, it was argued, put that radicalism at risk, just as scholars studying the organic and sustainable agriculture movements had revealed a progressive simplification and harmonization of standards as larger corporates sought certification on less onerous terms. Sales of certified products might grow but there is increasing concern that democratically run smallholder farmers will be pushed out of the Fairtrade loop as they find themselves incapable of meeting the quantities demanded by large corporations. Similarly, there is concern that big corporations are reluctant to spend time checking on isolated farms at the far end of the supply chain.

If alternative trade was nestling up to mainstream trade in order to increase sales, big agribusiness was also pulling out the stops – affordable stops – to align itself with lucrative social or ethical imperatives through well-worded corporate social responsibility policies and through certification systems that had more to do with brand profiles than with a long-term commitment to small co-operatives. Unless they have binding commitments to volume growth, such firms can 'burnish their corporate images' without really changing their practices. How transparent are their supply chains? What is their commitment to fair trade? What does it say about the 90-95 per cent of non-Fairtrade goods in their product ranges? What *is* fair trade if it is used by those that continue to conduct the vast majority of their business through conventional trading systems?

Because labeling is the key means of communicating fair trade claims, writes Daniel Jaffee, 'conferring the right to use the seal grants firms access to valuable branding real estate... This controversy over corporate "dabblers" participating in fair trade at allegedly token levels reflects a deeper divergence between the competing models of social change within the movement.'[3]

Originally applied to small agricultural co-operatives, the Fairtrade label has enabled large companies to benefit from the positive associations of fair trade, even though the bulk of their products is conventionally produced and traded and their commitment to long-term trading relationships appears minimal. Not only do these companies compete with small farmers – this time in the name of fair trade rather than free trade – but it also undermines the very enactment of fair trade.

Respondents in a Colorado State University survey reported a changing relationship with the fair trade movement as the alternative trade organization model has given way to labeling initiatives such as FLO. Interviewees characterized the new system as depersonalized and institutionalized, involving less frequent contact and, at times, insensitive and non-transparent communication. As the ethical trade campaigners Pedro Haslam and Nicholas Hoskyns have written: 'For those of us who founded fair trade as a tool for social change and revolution, it felt like betrayal. Despite considerable resistance, profound heart-searching and debate, they were included and started staking their certified fair trade products on to the shelves... The fair trade certified farmers who sell (to these transnational exporters) are back to being just farmers organized in first-level co-operatives, and are still locked into the traditional supply chains dominated by the largest companies. This is not the vision of sustainability and community many of us started out with, where local family-owned businesses sell the products of small farmers and personal relationships are maintained through the supply chain.'[4]

Plantation songs

Despite resistance from small producer groups and fair or alternative trading organizations, some plantation-grown items, such as tea, flowers and bananas (but not coffee or cocoa), are eligible for Fairtrade certification on the grounds that they are not available from smallholder operations. A precedent was seen to be set in 1996 when Europe's fair trade movement certified an African banana plantation that was 25-per-cent owned by a workers' trust. Today the Chiquita and Dole corporations, huge oligarchs of the world banana industry once mentioned in Human Rights Watch reports as labor rights violators, are found on the list of FLO-CERT registered traders. Yet Dole, for example, was the subject of lawsuits filed by hundreds of banana plantation workers in Latin America, Africa and the Philippines who claimed they suffered sterilization and other severe health problems from the pesticide Nemagon, which was banned in the US in 1979. As of 2012, Fairtrade-certified flowers, fresh and dried fruit, tea, sugar, cotton and spices are all sourced largely or entirely from plantations and estates.

The 'hired labor' provision of Fairtrade certification is a set of criteria distinct from the original small producer standards: employers must pay the national minimum wage, workers must have the right to organize (but the presence of independent unions is not required), and fair trade premiums are to be administered by a management-labor 'joint body'. As fair trade sales figures attribute the main source of growth to the agricultural plantation sector, results from fair trade impact studies, like those discussed in Chapter 3, tend to pall in analyses of certified plantations and estates. A number of media reports have uncovered situations where workers on certified estates are paid below national minimum wages, where TransFair and FLO-CERT are unable to monitor labor conditions effectively, where joint bodies are controlled by management and where unionization is virtually non-existent.

As Equal Exchange co-founder Rink Dickinson says: 'fair trade is for small farmers and small producers who are democratically organized. If you take the democracy out you have traditional aid or World Bank development or what the TransFair and the European certifiers are now trying to call fair trade. And fair trade is about access for those small producers. By slowly developing over time at significant risk, small farmers and producers can build solidarity networks and enter commercial supply chains. When they succeed at this there are benefits or positive development for their communities. That's what fair trade is all about.'[5]

Fair Trade USA splits

Tensions boiled over in 2004, when a group of 100-per-cent fair trade coffee roasters pulled out of the FLO-affiliated TransFair USA certification system, while committing themselves to remain fully fair trade and transparently auditable. By 2010, the majority of the 100-per-cent fair trade retailers in the US had left the FLO/TransFair system, with many of these shifting to a new certification system, Fair for Life, established by organic certifier IMO (Institute for Marketecology) and the Swiss Bio-Foundation to certify social account-ability and fair trade in agricultural, manufacturing and trading operations.

This was a timely departure. In 2011, Fair Trade USA (FTUSA, formerly TransFair USA) resigned its membership from Fairtrade International in preparation for its new initiative, Fair Trade For All. In meeting the goals implicit in this name, it plans to open certification to factory-made and plantation-grown products, even coffee. At the time of writing, FTUSA has three pilot projects, including the Fazenda Nossa Senhora de Fatima coffee estate in Brazil, where the new farmworkers' standard for coffee will be implemented and audited by independent certification company Scientific Certification Systems. As FTUSA president Paul Rice told Coffeelands blogger Michael Sheridan: 'It has two amazing owners who are pioneers of organics... Those owners have demonstrated a deep commitment to sustainability and to their workers. Fazenda is a natural fit for us.'[6]

According to its own literature, FTUSA will continue to evaluate impacts to ensure new producers are not displacing the sales of current co-operatives, but, as Daniel Jaffee notes, this move by FTUSA could permit large roasters such as Starbucks to become 100-per-cent fair trade certified 'without altering their supply chains'.[3]

Under the new FTUSA system, changes have also

been made to multi-ingredient product weightings. FTUSA requirements allow multi-ingredient products to carry the 'Fair Trade Certified' mark so long as they include a minimum dry weight of 25-per-cent fair trade ingredients. A 'Fair Trade Certified' chocolate bar, for example, could contain no fair trade cocoa whatsoever if its 25-per-cent sugar content was fair trade. Such policies make it difficult for consumers to distinguish between products with high fair trade content and those with minimal fair trade content, and between products made with ingredients grown by small farmer co-operatives and those using ingredients from 'fair trade' plantations. Again, economies of scale will inevitably kick in, making goods produced or grown in factories or plantations, where traditional fair trade standards of accountability, transparency, democracy and fair representation are harder to implement and audit, cheaper to buy, so further alienating small farmer operations.

The furore was instant. In 2012 Marike de Pena, Vice President of the Latin American and Caribbean Network of Small Producer Organizations (CLAC), wrote a public letter to the North American Fair Trade Council. Large-scale private-owned plantations, she wrote, are harmful to small producer organizations. They generate unfair competition as they have lower costs and more access to information, finance, technology and logistics:

'It is a lot easier, cheaper, faster and safer to buy from the big estates... Nobody cares any more about small farmers, whose incomes are far below workers' income, with no protection through any laws, no social security, no pension funds, no protection against climate change and no guarantee of markets. Plantations in Fair Trade did not enter to solve poor working conditions, rather, they entered to serve the market faster and cheaper. They create

unfair competition in Fair Trade, and will change the direction of Fair Trade to a charity movement and not a movement that supports farmers through empowerment and progress thanks to stable markets and sustainable prices; a movement that enables farmers to create progress through their own efforts and work... [The current changes] will exclude once and for all small farmers if we do not make the right decisions; if this happens, once again we will stop local community development and negatively impact good environmental practices: the market will win but the world will lose a unique system able to create change working with small organized farmers.'[7]

The World Fair Trade Organization responded to the FTUSA announcement with a similar sense of unease: 'We see little evidence of dialogue, transparency or respect (key aspects that define Fair Trade) in the unilateral decision of Fair Trade USA to widen the scope of Fair Trade in ways that will surely negatively impact those currently involved. This action seems more to satisfy and enrich the very people whose actions caused Fair Trade to be established in the first place, at the expense of the small farmer/producer.'[8]

No one denies the need for better pay and working conditions for plantation and estate workers as well as small farmers – for most of the 450 million waged laborers in agriculture, working conditions are grim. But the evidence to date shows state mechanisms and ILO conventions can be employed to monitor formal employment situations, and that, in supporting small, farmer-owned co-operatives, fair trade can provide a viable alternative to the more hierarchical systems of the plantation, industrial agriculture's 'single most bloody innovation'.[9] Certainly such moves fly in the face of recent findings that, as explained by UN Special Rapporteur on the Right to Food, Olivier De Schutter, 'achieving food security in developing countries requires increasing support to enhance the productive capacity of, and economic opportunities for, small-scale farmers.' As the report stated, there are approximately 500 million small-scale farmers in Majority World countries 'making them not only the vast majority of the world's farmers but, taking into account their families, responsible for the well-being of over two billion persons.'[10]

In effect, certification systems have changed fair trade to such an extent that sales of products have become the main measure of success instead of the welfare of producers. Fair Trade USA's move to certify plantations and factories, De Schutter says, 'helps to illustrate the point that there is no longer one easy definition of what fair trade is'.

Critics say this is one more step towards the complete involvement of corporates at every stage of international fair trade, from production through manufacturing to retailing – a corporate strategy better known as 'vertical integration'. Supporters argue that transnationals are needed for distribution and that mass-market coffee 'roastmasters' – a euphemism for the large coffee corporations that control the bulk of the global industry – will never bow to pressure from NGOs to support small farmer co-operatives. To increase sales of fair trade coffee, they argue, it is better to transform existing plantation suppliers to fit the 'fair trade' mold.

It is an age-old line of reasoning. If Muhammad (big business) won't go to the mountain (fair trade), the mountain must go to Muhammad. But there are real fears that, if it does so, fair trade standards will be compromised. Already much of the responsibility (and cost) for proving fair trade credentials is being pushed on to producer organizations, rather than being borne by buyers and distributors. There is also evidence that some certified groups are not really co-operatives but rather ghost co-operatives set up by large trading companies to meet Fairtrade requirements. There is also evidence that retro-certifying products allows buyers to purchase coffee at market prices and then pay the higher fair trade price to farmers only if their customers do first. And how strict will conditions of certification be? Already there are claims that minimum-entry purchase requirements have been dropped at the behest of large companies with big buying power.

Reading the fine print

The market for certification is growing. Bird-, forest-, marine-, environment- and worker-friendly labels swarm across supermarket shelves, each branded with their own goals and promises. Some of these are first-party certification labels, typically self-policing systems with no intermediary involved. Others are second-party codes implemented by enterprise-wide associations with monitoring through associated sector associations. Others again, like Fairtrade and Rainforest Alliance, are third-party codes monitored through external NGOs or certification bodies. Many producer organizations have more than one certification, giving them flexibility in selecting buyers and additional premiums. Faced with the plethora of labels and FTUSA's highly publicized breakaway from Fairtrade International, customers can be excused for feeling jaded. Marketplace fatigue is setting in. The finer details of Rainforest Alliance (used on McDonald's coffee), Fairtrade, Utz Kapeh, IMO, Geographic Labelling and Direct Trade are not widely understood. They all sound good but who is monitoring them? Who is writing the rules? And who is really benefiting?

The recent changes to fair trade certifying systems have forced the movement to look at its goals – should it be competing with other labels for increased market share? Or should it be working to give more authority and power to those who make or grow the goods it sells? Just as the first certification label was instigated not by a northern ATO but by a coffee-growing co-operative in the Global South, so producer organizations today are playing a larger role in the policies and decisions that have a major impact on their livelihoods. In November 2010, the Latin America and Caribbean Network of Small Fair Trade Producers and the Foundation of Small Organized Producers launched the new Small Producers' Symbol, an independent and affordable certification system based in countries of origin and built around the core values of sustainable production, democratic organization, fair trade and self-management. The goal: 'To differentiate ourselves as small producers that defend the original values of fair trade: co-operation, democratic governance, support for small farmer agriculture.'

Other symbols are appearing – organic certifiers Ecocert and IMO have created their own seals, Ecocert Equitable and Fair for Life respectively. Equal Exchange, AgroFair and Canada-based worker-owned co-operative La Siembra have worked to create small-farmer co-operative supply chains in the chocolate, tea and banana industries. In 2010, the Organic Consumers Association launched the Fair World Project to promote fair trade in organic production systems, and to protect the term 'fair trade' from 'dilution and misuse for mere PR purposes'. In 2013, the WFTO launched its own plans for a symbol to identify those products made or imported by 100-per-cent fair trade organizations. Unlike other certification systems, the cost will not be borne by the producers but rather by the buying or importing organization.

The purpose of all these new initiatives is to re-instate trust in 'authentic' fair trade, in a system that works on behalf of small farmers and producer organizations rather than being driven by buyers or traders who are able to push down prices or negotiate tough contractual arrangements. Fair trade does not have to go there. Critics of FTUSA's move say fair trade does not have to change the rules or bow to pressure to certify plantations.

This takes us back to Muhammad and his mountain. As fair trade strengthens, as it attracts further support by remaining true to its founding goals and responding to the needs of small farmer and artisan co-operatives and collectives, it has more chance of bringing corporates to it, on its terms, for the benefit of those fair trade was developed to support. 'So when TransFair says let's go get more volume in x, y, z commodity by talking to the businesses that already have volume so we can have impact,' says Equal Exchange co-founder Rink Dickinson, 'they have it 100-per-cent wrong.'[5]

Dickinson gives the example of tea, the first plantation-grown crop to be sold under Fairtrade accreditation and still a thorn in the side of many a fair trade supporter. Unlike coffee and cocoa, which are dominated by smallholder farms, tea has a long history of plantation or estate systems of production. So, when ATOs began looking for tea suppliers, they looked to plantations, not to any old plantation but to plantations nonetheless. Dickinson: 'It felt too hard to build an effective small farmer supply chain in tea, or bananas, so TransFair/FLO, over the repeated strong objections of the small-scale farmers who in fact created the fair trade seals in the first place, decided to introduce and then promote the idea of the fair trade plantation... Missing from this are small tea farmers. Not because there are none in Darjeeling. Because they lost the minute the beautiful fair trade idea built for them was mistakenly attached to a plantation that had no market access problem at all and completely dwarfed small farmers in resources.'

Equal Exchange chose not to go down that path. Just as it did with coffee – and even that, says Dickinson, was a long process – it is now working with small tea co-operatives. Support them, he says, and they are less likely to lose their farms and be forced to work on someone else's estate as a plantation laborer. But certifying plantations has caused another problem. By the time these small co-operatives have perfected their production and supply systems, by the time processing, exporting, financing and quality issues have been resolved, who will they sell to? ATOs have their plantation networks and even the big retail chains will say 'thanks, but we already have our suppliers'. Again, the small farmer is left in a no-win situation: 'Allowing plantations in took away market opportunities for small tea farmers and then the development that would occur from those opportunities,' says Dickinson. 'Fair trade plantation tea has completely stunted the path forward for small farmers in tea.'

Nor does certifying plantations deliver the social changes that characterize authentic fair trade. Unlike a successful farmer co-operative, a plantation is based on a hierarchy of land owners and employed workers. There is little wiggle room for added empowerment, control or decision-making.

In debating the FTUSA moves, Equal Exchange co-founder Jonathan Rosenthal wrote: 'If you choose to look at who is making this decision to radically change the imperfect tool called fair trade, you might admit that it is nearly totally driven by well-intentioned white folks in the US with lots of money and big dreams. The original idea of supporting the political and economic development process of organized small farmers has been tossed aside. The voice of those farmers and their organizations has been overridden in pursuit of this bigger dream. Change comes in many forms. To me, this feels like a move right out of the colonial playbook.' In a surprise ending to this playbook, FTUSA's dramatic rewriting of fair trade's founding philosophy may in fact be prompting an even more determined reaction to give the power of change back to those who have the most to lose – and to gain.[6]

1 ipsnews.net **2** organicconsumers.org **3** Daniel Jaffee, 'Weak Coffee: Certification and Co-Optation in the Fair Trade Movement', *Social Problems*, Vol 59, No 1 (Feb 2012). **4** Pedro Haslam & Nicholas Hoskyns, 'The Road to Freedom', in John Bowes (ed), *The Fair Trade Revolution*, Pluto Books, New York, 2011. **5** smallfarmersbigchange.coop/2011 **6** scottgsherman.com/investigations/fair-trade.php **7** smallfarmersbigchange.coop **8** nin.tl/ZoOOSL **9** Raj Patel, *Stuffed and Starved: Markets, Power and the Hidden Battle for the World Food System*, Portobello, London, 2007. **10** The World Trade Organization wto.org/english/news_e/news11_e/dedschutter_2011_e.pdf

7 Where to from here?

Fair trade has notched up some significant achievements. But, to continue to move forward, it has to up its game – to resist easy compromises and align itself with the small farmers and artisans that gave it life.

FAIR TRADE IS NOT a label. Not a list of criteria. Not a certification system. Rather it is a model and a work-in-progress. It provides market access to smallholder farmers and artisans on terms that support their transition from a position of vulnerability to one of strength and self-sufficiency. In working to meet this goal, fair trade's track record is generally positive – surveys show an overall improvement in income, and the benefits of co-operatization, training/education and affordable credit are widespread and deep-seated.

To achieve these goals, fair trade fought for its own 'policy space'. For many years it campaigned, lobbied, boycotted and petitioned against the behavior of the big brand names that dominated the commodities sector. At the same time, on behalf of its trading partners, it sought new buyers prepared to support a range of products on terms and prices that could be sustained by the market but could also change the lives of those who made or grew these products. And it succeeded on its own terms. Whereas in 1992 handcrafts accounted for 80 per cent of fair trade products, by 2002 the ratio had reversed in favor of agricultural products as fair trade made significant in-roads into supermarket stocklists and educated the buying public about fair – and unfair – trade. People listened to the stories and they bought the products. It took time, but this is what fair trade did, without watering down standards or turning its back on small farmer co-operatives. Not surprisingly, conventional trade took note. It sat up, paddled over, found a way to take a slice of the increasingly lucrative ethical bowl – on its terms.

Standing at the crossroads

Fair trade is at a crossroads. One path points to a pro-poor model of trade working solely and explicitly on behalf of the small farmers and artisans otherwise marginalized by global trading systems. The other is aimed at increasing sales of certified product, with the aim of bringing more farmers and workers into the ambit of fair trade. The two approaches have been variously defined as: idealist and realist; deep and shallow; mission-driven and market-based; transformer and reformer; innovator and imitator; outside (the market) and within. Each dichotomy provokes the same question. Is the goal of fair trade to establish an alternative system of global trade that empowers small producers in the Global South? Or is it to work within the conventional trading system to negotiate better-than-before terms of trade for all the world's commodity suppliers? Or, as the *New Internationalist*'s David Ransom puts it: 'Is the principal purpose of fair trade to change world trade; or will world trade change the principles of fair trade?'[1]

Dichotomy may be the wrong word. Whether working as an alternative trading organization with its own distribution network or operating within conventional markets by way of a certification label, fair trade and Fairtrade share certain principles that ensure, at the very least, a minimum price, mutually acceptable terms of trade and democratic representation. And between them they have grown a fringe, alternative initiative into an international system working in over 70 countries and clocking up sales of over $6.6 billion on behalf of more than 1.4 million farmers and artisans. One word or two, capitals or not, the movement has prompted customers the world over to question whom they are supporting with their shopping dollar and who grew or at least imported the coffee, tea or chocolate they buy. It has encouraged the formation of farmer co-operatives and artisan collectives. Access to credit has improved, community infrastructure has improved. Still in its infancy, fair trade has given the corporate heavyweights a run, if not for their money, then at least for their reputations. And it has shown governments and international institutions that they too have a mandate to fight for fairer trade rules. Fairtrade International CEO Harriet Lamb describes it as a win-win-win situation, using the example of Marks & Spencer's decision to sell Fairtrade-certified women's T-shirts: 'Sales rise. Reputation rises. It works for us, it works for them and it oh so clearly works for the farmers. Then it becomes a sustainable and virtuous circle which can begin to make Fairtrade the norm.'[2]

Such is the halo effect of Fairtrade. But is that halo going cheap?

The recent moves by FTUSA and the increasing involvement of large corporations that show no sign of extending their commitment to fair trade have alarmed many in the fair trade movement. Their main concern is that the slow movement towards more producer ownership of fair trade is being undermined just as it looks ready to expand. Jonathan Rosenthal wrote on the influential CRS Coffeelands blog that FTUSA 'captured decades of work done by a broad range of activists and then unilaterally changed the rules of the game'.[3]

Is it too late?

Is it too late for the fair trade movement to recover? As Pedro Haslam and Nicholas Hoskyns write: 'Fair trade has changed from a movement that effectively contributes to empowerment, social change and economic justice to one that is also effectively improving the image of some of the most mistrusted companies in the world. As a result of the debate surrounding the inclusion of multinationals and plantations the fair trade movement became divided and lost the unity of a shared vision. Instead the key players in fair trade have fragmented into many directions, in some ways setting the stage for the next wave of innovative fair trade developments.'[2]

Or as Santiago Paz, co-director of the CEPICAFE coffee farmer co-operative in Peru, more graphically put it: 'The car is speeding so fast, it's careening down the highway, and the certifiers haven't even noticed that the passengers – the small farmers – have all gone flying out the window.'[4]

The brakes are faulty. In thundering down this path fair trade risks reverting to the unequal market relations against which it has campaigned for so long.

Even the most ardent idealist/transformer/mission-driven innovator would not question the goal to draw more farmers and artisans into a system of trade that is open and transparent and ready to pay better than normal returns. But if this requires compromising standards and privileging larger, easier-to-control operations, then fair trade really has lost control of the car altogether. And for what? A temporary escalation of market share with an easy-to-procure add-on label that will inevitably lead to customer confusion, stagnating returns and farmer alienation.

You could say it is a failure of the movement. That in trying to be both a social movement and a certification system, it took its eye off the ball. That it was naïve to assume that corporate distributors would prioritize ethics over profits and not use its considerable muscle to insist on more amenable terms of 'fair' trade.

But the challenge now is clear and, if we build on past practice, achievable. I write this in a small café in earthquake-hit Christchurch, New Zealand/Aotearoa. For $20 at Black Betty café, home to locally roasted Switch Espresso, you can buy a small, leafy coffee plant. Of that sum, $5 goes to New Zealand fair trade organization Trade Aid, which uses the money to fund a coffee renovation program enabling partner co-operatives to replace ageing coffee trees (something coffee farmers often cannot afford to do because the cost is prohibitive). In the attached roastery, fair trade organic coffee beans are being prepared for the local café market.

Five years ago, Switch moved away from Fairtrade certification. 'I didn't like how the big corporates were using [Fairtrade] as a marketing tool for a very small percentage of their product,' says managing director Hamish Evans. 'I've always wanted to use fair trade as normal trade – and to some extent it has become the norm. Commercially we want a good quality product, good supply and good relationships. Organics brings in that quality and looking after the farmers brings in that quality. But you need to be able to trust your supplier. I have confidence trading through Trade Aid. Their standards are higher than Fairtrade's. If anyone asks where we get our coffee from I am happy to sit down and tell them about the amazing people we buy from.'[5]

This is what fair trade was built on – long-term trading relationships and a supply chain that is shorter, more transparent and more equitable than the systems of exchange orchestrated in London or New York or the practices of large agribusiness operations that patrol the globe looking for the lowest-priced commodities. From these roots fair trade can grow. In aligning with small farmers and artisans it does not have to restrict its activities to a small niche market. There are too many small farmer co-operatives and artisan groups to take that approach.

But nor does growth mean focusing on large plantations and estates. If we look around, we see evidence of growing South-South trade and the increasing role of producer co-operatives in running trading operations – a reversal of the vertical integration model described by academic Daniel Jaffee. Coffee co-operatives CEPCO and UCIRI have their own coffee shops in Mexico. The Bolivarian Alliance for the Peoples of the Americas (ALBA) is a regional agreement between Venezuela, Cuba, Bolivia, Nicaragua, Ecuador, Dominican Republic, Antigua, Barbados, and St Vincent and the Grenadines, aligning fair trade with food security and small farmer empowerment. Farmer co-operatives own shares in northern alternative trading organizations such as Cafédirect, Divine, Liberation, Etico and Equal Exchange, thereby having a role in making the decisions that affect their lives.

Tugging at the sleeves of corporate buyers was not part of the original plan. It was not why a group of indigenous Mexican coffee farmers in Oaxaca approached Dutch development organization Solidaridad with an idea for a new labeling system to identify its coffee in the marketplace. And it was not why Edna Ruth Byler hawked her small stock of Puerto Rican textiles from the trunk/boot of her car.

1 ipsnews.net/2008/11/ **2** Pedro Haslam & Nicholas Hoskyns, 'The Road to Freedom', in John Bowes (ed), *The Fair Trade Revolution*, Pluto Books, New York, 2011. **3** coffeelands.crs.org **4** cooperativegrocer.coop/article **5** Interview with the author 24 January 2013.

Index

Page numbers in **bold** refer to main subjects of boxed text and diagrams.

Index

Index